A
Split
Second
Accident.

A SPLIT SECOND ACCIDENT

MICK RINE

M A & D BOOKS
RAUNDS
NORTHANTS
2017

First Published 2017.

M A & D Books

ISBN 978 – 1 – 78808 - 550 – 2

Published by :
M A & D Books
47 London Road
Raunds
Wellingborough
Northamptonshire NN 9 6EH

michaelrine95@yahoo.co.uk

Printed and bound in Great Britain by
Lonsdale Direct Solutions
Denington Industrial Estate
Wellingborough
Northamptonshire NN6 9 BX.

Typeset in Constantia

FOREWORD

This biography tells the story of a young man who set off on his Lambretta Scooter, for an evening of Gymnastics training, at his School. During the training, he suffered a catastrophic injury, culminating in a long and complex hospitalization.

A few years later he decided to write a book about his life, but was unable to afford publication. His memoir was placed on a bookshelf, where it remained for many years.

In 2016 the Author Mick Rine read his younger brothers memoir and decided to update it and prepare it for publication. This book is dedicated to Alan.

CONTENTS.

PART ONE

The early life.

My name is Alan Rine and I was born in the borough of Hackney, London, in the winter of 1949. My parents were John and Rose Rine who lived in a rented three bedroomed house at 12, Aspland Grove, Hackney, London, E8. I was born at The Mothers Hospital, situated on Homerton High Street, Hackney. On leaving Hospital I was taken home to join my two older brothers David and Michael. As we grew up we all got on well as I recall and being a working class family, soon found boyhood jobs. In the main we worked on market stalls and also did paper rounds. The jobs provided us boys with some pocket money, which was not available from our parents.

The street that we lived in was in fact reasonably safe, being a Cul-de-sac, otherwise known as a 'dead end Street'. The children living in our Street could play games in the Street, there being very little passing traffic. Transport on the other hand was wrapped around us, with numerous London buses passing at the end of the Street. To the rear of our house was a steep railway embankment with three sets of railway lines, which were permanently in use by numerous steam locomotives. These in turn were pulling both passenger and goods trains, back and forth along the lines. I should perhaps mention, that when little boys became bored, we could always make our way up the embankment and sit watching the trains go by. Our parents of course were never to pleased to find us up the embankment, sat beside those fire breathing monsters.

None of the parents seemed to be particularly well off and this culminated in young children formulating their own plans for adventures. We would be found scrumping, bird nesting, tree climbing, swimming in the nearby canal and even jumping from canal bridges, into the murky water-below. We of course didn't know at the time that a number of dangerous items lurked just below the surface of the water. Examples would be old rusting bikes, cars, assorted debris and even sunken boats and barges. I'm pleased to say that all of our friends and family managed to avoid these hidden obstructions, more by luck, than judgement.

On a safer note we all managed to hackle together various pedal bikes, which were then used both in the street and for adventures beyond Hackney. We started cycling to places like Whips Cross, Woodford, Chingford and of course Epping forest. The main objective was to be out in the air and out in woodland and countryside. Talking very plainly, we needed to be well away from the hustle and bustle of good old Hackney. It of course had it's dangers and sadly as we walked on one occasion, a girl by the name of Margaret Ferris was knocked down by a car, at Whips Cross. Unfortunately she was rather knocked about and spent a short period of time at the local hospital.

I would say that I was quite astute from an early age and managed to save most of my pocket money by means of Post Office Saving Stamps. Dad was a very sensitive individual and found it hard to keep a job for longer than a week or so. Mum on the other hand worked very hard indeed at home on her sewing machine. She was referred to as a rag trade worker, making silk linings for the clothing industry. Mum was one of many women working at home for mainly Jewish entrepreneurial factory owners, in and around Hackney.

As I grew up my parents had four more children, resulting in a family total of seven children. There is little doubt that my Mum was responsible for keeping our family together. It's a sad thing to say, but had we relied on Dad, I'm confident in saying that some of our number would have ended up in Children's Homes. For the uninformed, Hackney was one of more than fifty Borough's that made up The greater London area, which had a population of over 8 Million people. It was a very big city to grow up in and was constantly congested, with all forms of traffic. On a bright note there was always plenty to do and always places to go. Cinema's and swimming pools were in abundance, as were the number of parks to play in. Children growing up in London were never short of options, when it came to using up their spare time.

I became a strong swimmer mostly due to the fact that Hackney swimming baths was just around the corner. By the age of thirteen I had perfected four powerful strokes namely Crawl, Breast stroke, Back stroke and Butterfly. In the summer time my friends and I would swim at the open air Lido at London Fields. These were great times for young school boys, because we could show off to various girls who were in attendance from our school. I also became a keen gymnast and regularly attended evening classes at my senior school, which was funded by The Greater London Council.

At the age of sixteen I had passed a good number of GCE examinations and was now preparing for "A" levels. These preparations related to Mathematics, Science and English Language, all needed, with a view to joining The Royal Air Force. I'm afraid I was stopped in my tracks with this ambition when it was discovered that I suffered with colour blindness. Coupled with my "A" level studies at evening time was a tendency to visit The Britannia Pub, in Mare Street, Hackney for a pint or two of Red Barrel beer. I had become of age, well nearly, and the Red Barrel rounded off the evening rather nicely. The Britannia by the way was positioned right next door to "The Hackney Empire" For the uninformed this was one of the finest examples, of our famous Music Halls.

I would now like to tell you a little about my older brothers, David and Michael, who, after leaving School, were both doing 5 year apprenticeships, the former in carpentry and the latter in engineering. David liked to frequent our local pub ' The Earl of Amhurst ' and played darts, with the pub team. Michael was a little more adventurous and had reached a grade of ' Green belt ' at Judo lessons, which were held at a nearby School, called Upton House. They had both attended my Secondary Modern School, called 'Hackney Free and Parochial ', which had been built in Paragon Road, Hackney. In the fullness of time, as a result of day release from their employers, they attended technical college and both received City and Guilds Diploma's, at first class level.

At the age of seventeen I had saved sufficient pocket money to buy myself a Lambretta Scooter. With the appropriate ' L' plate in place. I had started taking driving lessons and life was feeling ' pretty good'. A couple of my friends also had Scooters and trips out were being planned. We had all purchased Parka coats, which of course, were worn with pride. We did not see ourselves as 'mods' who were of course prominent at that time. We certainly did not want to fall out with any 'rockers' either. We were very much aware of the huge bikers club in Hackney, The infamous ' 59 ' club, which incidentally was based close to my school. On occasions, as many as two thousand bikers would descend upon the club, with rock and roll, in mind.

My life at this particular time was just great. 'The world was my oyster'. I had mates, a bike, money in the bank, good health, youth on my side and last but not least, a great future ahead of me. Colour blindness had of course become a nuisance, with my first career choice, but three good ' A ' levels would certainly help towards my next career choice. I didn't have a single clue, as to what my second career choice might be! I had plenty of time to formulate plans for my second career choice and decided simply to enjoy life, in the interim!

Now seems to be the right moment to introduce the reader to a rather limited photograph of Hackney Free and Parochial, Secondary modern, school. The school was built in Paragon Road, Hackney and this particular photograph depicts the typical red brick used in its construction. This part of the building was situated slightly left of the main entrance of the School.

A Split Second Accident

PART TWO – LIFE CHANGING.

Black Monday.

After a weekend off from school, Monday had arrived, with an uneventful day at school. Evening had arrived and it was time to make my way back to school for my gymnastics classes. I rode my scooter the short distance to Hackney Free and Parochial Secondary Modern School and parked up in the teachers car park. I then went to the changing rooms and got changed into my PE kit, before joining my fellow gymnasts, in the school gymnasium.

The plan that evening was to perfect somersaults in preparation for a future display. This involved using a trampet, a small trampoline with a spring area of some three foot square. We took turns running up to the trampet, bouncing off it into the air and landing squarely on our feet, on the matting on the other side. After a couple of good somersaults, I prepared for a third attempt. This was now the moment which would change my life for ever. I ran up to the trampet, bounced off into my flip, and as I straightened out, my feet just skimmed the mat and passed under me. This caused the upper part of my body and my vulnerable chin, to smash hard into the matting. My head was forced violently back and up, and it was just as if an unseen giant had ruthlessly taken me by the ankles and smashed my head, chin first onto the floor.

During the split second the floor had come up to meet me, I had instinctively thrust my arms out in an effort to break my fall, but as my hands hit the mat, my arms were forced into a bent attitude due to the speed at which I came out of the spin. Looking back, I believe that there was absolutely nothing I could have done to avert the way I landed, during that fearful split second. I was severely shocked, but still conscious and I immediately cried out when I realised I was unable to move. I was flat on my front, with my arms positioned as if I were about to perform a press up, and my head was extended fully back with my chin resting on the mat.

The instructor assumed I couldn't move due to shock, but he decided to call for an ambulance in case I was more severely injured. Yet, although no one knew, least of all me, I had completely smashed two of the vertebrae in my neck, these simultaneously cutting deep into my spinal cord running centrally down the inside of the vertebral column. Yes, I had broken my neck. Apart from the mild pain I felt there, I had the odd sensation that my legs were somehow floating skywards. However, the instant the instructor returned from phoning for the ambulance, I mentioned that I was having difficulty breathing and he agreed when I asked to be rolled over onto my back. Others then assisted the instructor in turning me onto my back, at which point the ambulance crew arrived.

It was at that point that I recall feeling as though my legs were then doubled up beneath me through an invisible hole in the floor. This was strange to say the least because I could see my legs stretched out straight in front of me, on the mat. The ambulance men then listened to what had happened and one of them produced a large pin which he then thrust into the soles of my feet. As he did this I felt no pain at all in my soles. The ambulance crew seemed to know more about my situation, than they were prepared to state. Some of the boys present were then instructed by the ambulance crew, as to how they could help to place me onto the stretcher.

Once on the stretcher I was very carefully carried down the stair case and out of the gym area to the ambulance. The ambulance set off at a very slow pace and it took an age to reach Hackney Hospital. The driver drove very carefully with a view to avoiding any unnecessary jolts to my body. On arrival at the hospital I was gently transferred to the casualty department to await examination. Meanwhile my gym instructor had driven over to my home to inform my parents of my mishap. He returned to the hospital shortly afterwards with my mother at which point a doctor started to examine me.

The doctor then asked me what had happened at the gym. I explained in detail, including how I now felt. The doctor then asked me to raise my left leg, but despite my best effort I couldn't raise it. He then made the same request with my right leg and again I couldn't raise it. It was then strongly suggested that I wasn't trying hard enough. I told the doctor that I was trying extremely hard to comply with his requests, but was completely unable to raise either leg. The doctor then requested that I move each of my arms in turn. I was now becoming upset because I couldn't move my arms or indeed my hands. He then asked me to form a fist with each hand in turn. Again despite my best concentration I could not make a fist with either hand.

From then on, an endless line of doctors came in the department to see me and it was decided that I should have some neck X-rays taken. Whilst in the X-ray department I was held in many an odd position for some good shots to be taken. My head was not kept in any one position, under the assumption that my neck was actually broken. Thus, although ignorant of it then, a great part of the damage sustained on my spinal cord may well have been inflicted when the X-rays were being taken. I feel that limited knowledge of spinal injury was available in General Hospitals at the time of my accident.

Eventually the hospitals most eminent orthopaedic consultant saw the x-rays and concluded that I should attend the operating theatre forthwith. Yet, to my great surprise, I was about to under-go a far stranger ordeal than an every day operation. Whilst in the outer theatre I became acutely embarrassed for the first time in my young life, when I discovered that the nurses were to remove my shorts and shirt. To avoid moving me they snipped my shirt up the middle

and then slipped my shorts off, when for a few
scarlet moments I was left completely in my
birthday suit! It may seem daft but the more I
thought about my state of undress, the more
flushed I became and the nurses were all highly
amused.

A little later, adorned in a beautifully white
theatre gown, they wheeled me under the theatre
arc lights where a chap came and asked me to relax.
He said he was going to remove a little hair from
above each ear and, in fact, a great deal of my hair
was removed, followed by the shaving of these two
areas with a safety razor. Next, an anaesthetist
introduced himself and explained he was about to
give me a local anaesthetic in the top of my head,
for the surgeon to be able to work there.

When the surgeon arrived, he produced
nothing less daunting than a carpenters brace and
bit. Assuming he was going to drill a hole in my
head with it, I timidly asked him just what was
about to happen, but he merely told me to lie still,
that it wasn't going to hurt, and that I would soon
be out of the theatre. Well, having only been given
a local anaesthetic, I was able to observe his actions
and when I realised just what he was doing, I
wished to high heaven I'd had a general anaesthetic

instead! The surgeon raised the brace and bit up to the side of my head and drilled a hole into my skull. The hole was drilled on the side of my head where the hair had earlier been removed. He then carried out an identical procedure culminating in a second hole being drilled in the same position, but on the opposite side of my scull. It was explained to me that these small holes had both been drilled to a certain necessary depth. This was quite a shocking experience to say the least. I didn't suffer any real pain but could hear the drill bit doing it's job of work.

The surgeon then simultaneously screwed something into each of the aforementioned holes, which I later learned to be a pair of head traction calipers. As the screws were turned, I sensed the vibration throughout my head. I was now entering into a new world of spinal injury treatment and medicine. I found this first procedure to be quite shocking, but was soon to learn how very necessary it was for both me and many, many other patients. When someone breaks their neck the vertebrae are usually severely smashed and splintered and for the bones to be healed reasonably straightly, the head must be pulled out and the neck extended. This is why the calipers are screwed securely into the skull,

providing a good anchor point for the attachment
of the necessary weights, which are later fixed to a
head caliper cord. Thus, the traction is provided for
straightening out the bones during the healing
period. Whilst lying prone in the horizontal plane,
the traction weights are tied onto the opposite end
of a cord, which is attached to the calipers from
just above the head.

All very complicated I'm sure you'll agree, but
not all broken necks are treated in this way, as
some of the breaks are far less serious than others.
There are many degrees at which a neck can be said
to have been broken. Some people may be classed
as having sustained a broken neck, which in fact is
only a hairline fracture. In this situation a harness
under the chin type of traction would probably be
fitted, or even just a stiff collar would be worn until
the fracture had healed. In such cases the
individual concerned would very likely get away
without sustaining any permanent degree of
paralysis.

Unfortunately in my case the lesion to the
spinal cord seemed fairly extensive and the doctors
accordingly decide to apply a semi-permanent set
of head traction calipers, which were considered
the best way of fixing one's head correctly for the

relatively long term necessary. Remarkably, numerous people actually know very little about the most important bone in their body, with the spinal cord system passing directly through it. In the passing of time, I would often be asked why, if the bones in one's previously broken neck had healed, does a person such as myself, become permanently disabled and confined to a wheelchair for life? Well, I now know the answer in that it is important to understand that it is broken or dislodged vertebrae bones which cause paralysis by their pressing against or cutting into the spinal cord nerves.

The bones will subsequently heal and any bruising to the cord will eventually go down, but the nerves of the spinal cord itself will be left at approximately that degree of damage sustained at the time of the accident. These nerves do not heal up or regenerate themselves, as do the peripheral nerves in one's limbs. These casualties are likely to be left permanently paralysed, because there is no known means, as yet, of putting them right.

It may well be asked, why do the doctors not operate to remove any bone splinters or vertebrae that may be causing pressure to the spinal cord? Well, it is because the nerves themselves are accepted to be so delicate that any such operation could easily result in the person sustaining further paralysis during the operation. On the other hand if a surgeon was reasonably sure that the paralysis was being caused by a vertebrae or two exerting pressure to the cord, he might well go ahead with such an operation. However having been fitted out in my peculiar looking head gear, I was wheeled off to another part of my new world, a ward where I was to spend my next few days of hospitalisation.

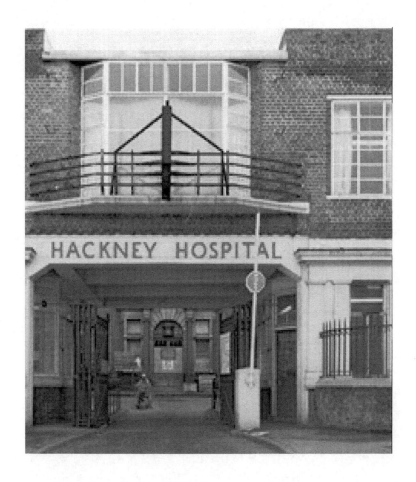

This photograph depicts the front
entrance to Hackney Hospital.

The Stryker frame.

In the ward I was transferred onto a bed which was like a medieval torture rack and it most certainly felt like one. The stryker frame had been invented for people suffering spinal injuries.
 A patient could be laid upon it and it was then unnecessary for him to be moved out of the lying down position, cutting out any risk of causing further injury to the neck or backbone fracture. It takes a long time for a fracture to heal well and since the patient has to spend this healing period in bed without being moved, he or she is very prone to developing bed sores. The patient will probably be unable to move anyway, due to paralysis and therefore has to be regularly turned by the hospital staff. On an ordinary bed all this turning could be rather dangerous, possibly causing extra damage to the fracture or to the spinal cord lesion.

Initially the turns should be carried out approximately every two hours to prevent the patient developing any bed sores, but as time passes the skin toughens and one can eventually be left in any one position for anything up to eight hours at a stretch. However, it should be noted that this longer turning time can only be adopted by those who have been paralysed for some years.

When I lay on the stryker frame I was turned every two hours and at almost at every turning an audience gathered to watch what was considered to be a rather novel process, although their pleasure was not shared by me, as can only be imagined.

The frame had been designed, so that the whole part the patient was lying on, could be swivelled through an axis in the horizontal plane. Just above my head a pulley wheel had been attached to the stryker frame and the cord which had been tied to my head calipers passed over this pulley wheel. This cord then stretched downwards within a few inches of the floor, at which point weights were attached to it. I had eight pounds of traction weights to begin with, but some people needed more weight and others needed less.

The appropriate weights were calculated to pull the neck out, into a suitable position for healing, against the pull of their neck muscles. One chap I later met, had to have some sixteen pounds attached, due to his particularly well developed muscles. I recall thinking, rather him than me and that eight pounds was more than adequate.

The actual turning process was carried out by two to three nurses and I recall thinking that they had probably never carried out this procedure before. They made me feel like the original human Guinea pig. To turn from lying on my back to lying on my front, these well meaning nurses had to affix an identical framework to the one under my body, to the bed above me. They would then revolve the whole stryker frame through one hundred and eighty degrees on its axis. In theory I the patient should then end up face down, lying on ones front. However, I believe the engineer who had designed the frame, hadn't taken into account the fact that quadriplegics were unable to control arm movement. Every time that I was turned my arms dropped downwards and of course became jammed in the work. Although no damage was sustained it was rather frustrating for both the patient and the nurses concerned. After the turn the frame above me could be temporarily detached, until the time came for it to be replaced ready to spin me back onto my back.

I really came to dread the coming of another turning time, whenever I was to go face down again, as my face was then rested into a canvas with a hole in the middle, which caused my chin to become very sore and my eyebrows to puff up. It was extremely frustrating whenever there was anyone to talk to because you couldn't see who it was. On a bright not whenever my mother visited I seemed to be positioned on my back and its always great to be able to see and hear your mum!

Eating was generally a problem, but even more so when lying on your front. The earlier mentioned canvas made it virtually impossible to move your lower jaw and I had to move my head to be able to chew at all. I ate very little at the time because it was both awkward to swallow whilst lying flat and after eating I would often feel like vomiting. My mouth and lips became cracked which was another good reason for not wishing to eat. We were given a jelly substance for the mouth and lips, but it tended to dry to quick and it of course had a nasty taste.

The whole eating and drinking problem presented a headache for my doctors, because my type of injury was relatively rare and they didn't appear to be sure as to whether or not my body could still handle food and liquids. A patient with a severe spinal cord lesion not only loses control of his legs, or legs and arms, but very probably his control of the trunk muscles that would normally have functioned by way of the nerves lying below the level of the spinal cord damage. A patient can become completely incontinent and my doctors, not knowing whether I was incontinent or not were in two minds, about me eating and drinking normally. They had concerns about my bowels and bladder becoming overly full. Not being medically educated, I nevertheless thought I understood their concerns. Ha Ha.

On a brighter note, soon after my admittance, arrangements were made for me to enter a specialist hospital near Aylesbury, Buckinghamshire. My doctors at Hackney had detailed discussions on the phone with spinal Injury Specialists at Aylesbury, who concluded that I could have light meals until I was transferred to them. They advised that I be given a very low fluids diet as the bladder can rapidly become overfull, resulting in renal back flow complications, due to one's being incapable of passing water.

I discussed my injury with a charge nurse, who painted what I regarded as a very grim picture. I asked him how long he thought it might be before I would be able to resume my schooling and when he estimated some six months or more, I raged that this was far to long a time to have to waste, as I had to get back to my examination Studies. Yet when he attempted to console me, by saying that I could take exams any time, I was still very unhappy, as I couldn't appreciate just why I had to waste an entire six months before being able to get back to school.

I had of course been working very hard on my ' A ' level subjects and despite my new situation, I, believe it or not, could not get my head round the fact that studies had now come to an almighty stop. I was now realising that I was going to be in a constantly prone position and totally incapable of reading or writing. In that split second, I had gone from being a very capable individual to being totally incapable of doing anything, without help from others. I can tell you that this realisation is simply enormous, particularly for someone so young.

Clearly, I just didn't understand how serious my condition was, because my mother had already been confidentially informed that I was on the danger list. The medical facts were that I had fractured two vertebrae classified as being c5 and c6. The letter C signifies cervical, which in layman's terms means neck bones, with the upper most seven vertebrae of a spinal column being cervical parts. So if you injure any of these seven vertebrae, you are a cervical classification. My c 5 had been crushed against my c 6 resulting in a c 5 / c 6 lesion.

At the level of c 4 or above, one's breathing is affected because the nerves connected to the spinal cord at that level operate the diaphragm. Had the bruising to my spinal cord worsened following the accident, it could well have affected my c4 area and I could have stopped breathing and this was one of the reasons that I had been placed on the danger list. Had I stopped breathing the doctors would have inserted a trachea tube or breathing pipe into my wind pipe at throat level to allow me to breath. I later learned that numerous casualties similar to my self had undergone this procedure.

I had been placed on the danger list due to damage to my central nervous system, which causes massive shock and may have resulted in my whole system collapsing. On a bright note my bruising didn't worsen and it was agreed that I should be transferred to Stoke Mandeville Hospital for further treatment. I had never heard of this hospital before, but I was certainly going to know all about it, in very quick time. I recall my brothers David and Michael coming in to see me and both

being very shocked at what had happened to me.
Michael mentioned that he had sustained an injury
the same evening as me, by breaking his little toe at
his Judo club. This struck the whole family as being
a very strange coincidence, in that we had both
ended up in a casualty department, at the same
time.

After 4 days at the Hackney Hospital I was
told that I was to be transferred to my next
Hospital by helicopter. I must say that despite my
dilemma I looked forward to this coming new
experience, I refer to – the ride in the helicopter of
course.

Flying high.

I was handled like eggs when I left Hackney
Hospital to fly to Stoke Mandeville. The nursing
staff wheeled me gently down to the ambulance
that was to convey me to the helicopters location. A
charge nurse was appointed to accompany me on
the trip in case I developed any complications
during the flight, a not unreasonable precaution
considering my temperature had been hovering

around the 103 mark! Although most cases experience a post accident lowering of temperature, my high temperature was put down to the fact that my neck had been broken backwards. The vast majority of neck breaks were caused by a forward moving break.

I was still on a fluid diet, but some ice cubes had been supplied to moisten my mouth and lower my temperature. I felt rather rough in the ambulance bay, but I was given a mental boost by the cheery send off by the staff. One particularly attractive nurse from my ward said goodbye, and as men do, I recall making a definite mental note to 'chat her up' when I was fit and well enough, to do so. I'm proud to say that I was being very optimistic. I suppose the real truth of my condition had still not wholly sunk in, despite all the warning signs.

I was still attached to my stryker frame and the ambulance had been completely stripped, to accommodate awkward customers like me. An ambulance officer had arrived to supervise matters and he checked that ambulance out inch by inch, to ensure himself and I, that the frame couldn't slip it's anchors.

What a fuss they made, I found myself laughing at such stringent care and precaution. I had the giggles and forgot about the ice cube in my mouth, which I nearly choked to death on. The ambulance had been provided with a Police escort, to ensure safety over the half mile trip to the landing area, which was at the local playing fields. We made a cautious start along the road, downhill at about five miles an hour. I recall my charge nurse and ambulance man were in stitches over the bewildered looks of bystanders and passing motorists. It appeared that these people just couldn't understand why this particular ambulance should need to go so slow. Furthermore, the question why had a Police escort been in attendance?

I of course couldn't observe what had been happening, because I was on my back, fixed by my traction, staring at the ceiling. This however provided me with an opportunity to see what I looked like in a head traction unit, as the shiny white roof of the ambulance served as a mirror. My image was somewhat distorted and I decided that I looked like the devil himself with large horns protruding above my ears. There was nothing particularly attractive about my calipered self and the sight made me feel somewhat despondent over what people thought of my new look. Yes, no matter what the situation there's always time for a bit of vanity, but it's strange that I should be more concerned with my general appearance than what was actually wrong with me.

Frankenstein's monster would have been proud of me, comparing that huge bolt passing through his neck, with the calipers that seemed to pass directly through my brain, from one side of the head to the other. As for my hair, it looked as though someone had used a knife and fork on it, especially those two patches by my ears. Even so, it harassed me and during that short trip down to the playing fields, I recall wondering if all this wasn't some form of divine retribution for all my past iniquities. These melancholy thought's quietly dispelled however, as we arrived at the playing fields. The ambulance doors were swung open and because my helicopter trip had been publicised on radio, a small crowd had gathered but luckily no one asked me to sign autographs.

The helicopter stood by for me, whilst standing by for the helicopter was a large red fire-engine, just in case anything went wrong. Some firemen gave a hand over the grassy area and into the chopper, which was of an air sea rescue type. The loading platform proved to be a little high, but with the assistance of the fireman I was raised up and placed in the helicopter. The whole team made sure that the stryker frame was kept square throughout the loading process. To my relief they prevented any nasty tugging on my neck, which of course was still being held in place by the caliper and considerable weights. What price vanity, I could see TV cameras angled in on me and the press were there too. Apparently some of the national dailies were publishing short articles on my situation.

The frame was well tied down and we were all set to go. I was a little apprehensive as this was to be my first trip into the wide blue yonder. I said goodbye to my Mother and recall thinking what on earth would she be making of all this. Mum then promised me that she would visit me as soon as possible, after I had settled in at Stoke Mandeville. The door was then closed and the rotors whirred. I could sense the moment when the chopper lifted off the ground, it then dipped a little as we hovered momentarily over the ground. In my humble opinion the pilot was very competent and he kept the chopper on an even keel. There was nothing he could do about the awful noise created by the helicopter blades. I simply couldn't make myself heard, so I decided to just try and relax whilst sucking on an ice cube. Air pockets became troublesome and the ups and downs on the trip were reminiscent of fair ground big dippers. Fortunately my stomach behaved quite well!

All things considered I enjoyed the trip, despite its short duration. It only took fifteen minutes to complete the forty mile journey, which ended as it begun in another playing field. We were duly greeted by an amiable doctor, who welcomed me and assisted in my removal from the chopper. I remember very clearly being wheeled across a rough surface into the Stoke Mandeville Complex. I was to see the playing field area numerous times in the future, but I never used it as I had been used to using such fields, prior to my accident. I hope I'm not giving to much away at this early stage in my journey.

Pin pricks and Things.

My first impressions of Stoke Mandeville Hospital.

Well, first the smell of the carbolic acid wavering around the swimming pool, as I was wheeled in. Secondly the overpowering smell of boiled greens as I was wheeled into Ward 2x, yes, it was lunch time.

Still, I soon forgot about these obnoxious things when I was liberated from my stryker frame and gently placed on what seemed to be a large flat bed. This made more than a pleasant change, I assure you, even though my head traction came along with me; but I wasn't allowed to enjoy my ' freedom ' for long, as a Doctor arrived immediately to check me over. A full assessment of my condition was to be made. Acting on information received from Hackney Hospital the doctor proceeded in his bid to discover the exact extent of my paralysis.

The doctor explained that there were two main sets of nerves running down the inside of the spinal column – the motor power and the sensory. There is a third set however – the autonomic, outside of, but actually connected to the cord, which is relevant to the extent that, it is usually also damaged in a spinal injury accident, causing loss of bowel and bladder control.

To assess my motor power or moving power damage, the doctor simply had to ask me to attempt to move either of my limbs, wriggle my toes, or form a fist with either hand. I was unable to carry out any of the movements requested and the doctor could see no physical response, apart from a little shoulder movement! The doctor stated that my motor power or movement functioning appeared to be 90% ' Kaput '.

The doctor then moved onto assessing sensory damage, which he explained was a slightly more difficult process. This involved pain, touch, vibratory and involuntary responses. I was then pin-pricked dozens of times from my toes up to my chin, having been asked to report where I felt the pin sharp, blunt or not at all. To ensure that I wasn't cheating the Doctor occasionally turned his pin around and used the head of the pin. Call-my-bluff with a vengeance! I felt it either sharply or bluntly on my right toes, my right inside thigh, right groin, right breast and inside upper right arm.

The Doctor then worked his way from bottom to top again, touching with a piece of fluff which I felt on my right toes, my inside thighs, my buttocks, groin, breast and inside upper arms. From just above my nipples my feeling was normal. Next came the vibratory test which involved the doctor striking a tuning fork and placing it on various bones to discover where I could sense vibrations, but alas I could only detect it on my right foot and right hip bone. Finally, he checked for involuntary responses – rather like those leg cross and tap physical fitness tests, we've all seen on hospital programmes. He also took a blood sample and asked me to blow as strongly as I could into a gadget which measured lung capacity.

All of the above finally drew the doctor to the conclusion that I was a high c 5/6 complete motor power – incomplete sensory. At that point I began to think what on earth does all this jargon mean for a 17 year old casualty. Well, the doctor then cheered me up, stating "Had you been an incomplete motor power and complete sensory you might have been able to operate a few muscles. Still, this meant little to me, so I asked the doctor whether this news was good or bad. He replied quickly, stating that it was yet early days and my situation could improve after any bruising to the Spinal cord had gone down.

Whilst chatting to both staff, fellow patients and visitors I was rapidly learning a lot about varying degrees of spinal injury,
 for example:- An injured spinal cord alone would mean a minimum three months lie in bed, flat out, until the fractured bones had sufficiently healed, This would be followed by a rehabilitation course, when up, to adapt one's future life to a wheelchair, a set of crutches, or, if ... in luck, even to walking again!

A road accident spinal case, however, might have sustained multiple injuries, and any flesh wounds could easily become bad pressure sores if the ward staff were not informed of their existence. Casualties with numerous flesh wounds would be placed on ' bed packs ', a number of small sections of mattress so arranged as to leave gaps between the mattress sections and thus avoid pressure to the injured parts.

A lot of juggling around was necessary for such cases, each time they were turned over and I remember one unfortunate young man who had to spend almost six months in bed on such packs before he was able to get up, because he had completely stripped the flesh off his backside in a motor cycle accidental backside pressure when up would have resulted in a very nasty pressure sore, so he to stay put until it had completely healed. Prior to this patients dilemma, I had already formulated the view that I had arrived at Stoke Manderville-for the long haul. As things quietened down in respect of my reception at Stoke Mandeville, I found myself dwelling on my new predicament. In everyday conversation, I had heard people refer to doing things at ' break neck speed ', well, I now clearly understood exactly what that meant. A split second accident had occurred and from that moment onward a considerable amount of treatment had been administered to me, both at Hackney and Stoke Mandeville, hospitals. I had until now, lost all sense of time and now had a moment to reflect on my situation. I suddenly realised that I was completely unable to do anything physical for myself. On the limited plus side, I could see, hear and speak. Also, with a little help from my friends, namely hospital staff, I could also eat and drink. It was quite a realisation, the moment when you realised what limited ability, you had left as a result of an accident.

Turning again.

Having served my apprenticeship on a stryker frame, I was now graduated to one of the latest wonder turning beds which had recently been introduced into the wards of Stoke Mandeville. I was still to be regularly ' turned ' in order to avoid the development of those wretched sores which are brought about by one's lying too long on tender spots in any one position. A jovial ward sister assured me I would find this electrically operated device a marked improvement on the stryker frame and I had to take her word for it until I discovered differently. As an extra precaution against the development of sores three pillows were positioned under my legs, hips and chest to extremely good effect and there was a further one placed between my legs and another to support my feet.

Thus, I was tilted, angled and partially sandwiched by this remarkable contraption from one turn time to another, but it still had the characteristics of a medieval torture rack, especially where my head was supported by a steel contraption, slotted into place on the bed frame. Where my ear and face came into contact with this head support, the metal was covered by white leather padding which had been too solidly packed, causing me to become sorer by the minute.

A four hour period of immobility like this could make one mentally 'sore' as well. So its no wonder I had to move my head now and again in order to alleviate the nagging pain in my ear and face, even though we had been cautioned that it was very unwise to attempt to do this. Many, many times when the side head support was in place, my head traction was accidentally knocked, sending vibrations reverberating through my skull. In addition to this sometimes my head would slip off the pillow, and as the metal calipers struck the metal head support my whole head would be set off vibrating again. It developed into a vicious circle, as with my skull holes being unable to heal with the metal inserted into them, they would be continuously made to bleed and weep with every little knock the calipers received.

I felt very low as the days progressed and my face and ears became increasingly sore, but there was a much more subtle torture in the offing when parts of me started to itch and I couldn't do anything about it. Imagine being able to move but the tiniest fraction when your nose begins to itch. You wriggle your nose, you blow from your mouth, and you try to reach it with your tongue. All to no avail. Then the ward staff rustle by, all far to busy to heed your pleas for a scratch. The blankets tucked up to your chin then begin to take an increasingly claustrophobic effect, as you desperately attempt to move your paralysed arms. You try again, wriggle, blow, lick or any permutation of the three. Someone, please, before my mind blows into gibbering little pieces – help me. And just as you are lapsing into insanity, a ministering Angel gives you a short, sweet scratch on your troublesome nose, and for one divine moment you glimpse what its like to be in heaven.

I feel for the time being, that you the reader of this rather fine book, has suffered enough with my details of a patients bed life, at Ward 2x.

My therapeutic friend.

On the second morning after my arrival, I was introduced to my physiotherapist. A physio is appointed to a patient and he or she will then treat that patient for the whole period he or she is in the hospital. And this, of course, enables the therapist to become well acquainted with her charge. The

majority of physio staff at Stoke Mandeville were
female and suited many of us males right down to
the ground. They were a great psychological
comfort to people such as myself since we could
regularly discuss the medical ins and outs, whilst
enjoying their proximity.

Physio's who were new to the hospital and
new to spinal injuries, could be rather a strain on
the new patients by putting them through an
everlasting interrogatory third degree. A new case
with a new physio wasn't exactly an ideal
combination, but the longer serving physio's were a
tremendous source of encouragement both to old
and new cases alike. Yes, it came as a very welcome
surprise for a male patient to discover he suddenly
had a new and attractive friend and I always
sympathised with the female sufferers who could
not enjoy the benefit of having a male physio to
attend to theirs needs.

I don't want to give a wrong impression, but
any sexual activity when suffering the early stages
of paralysis, was very unlikely. I suppose fantasy
played an enormous part in our recovery, whatever
your sexual orientation might be. Your everyday
thoughts had to include some pleasure and if this
meant a fantasy about your physio then ' lets do

this ' I'm afraid one's choices were very limited. Our capability in this particular arena was very limited indeed.

Of course, not all of the physio staff were young and beautiful, but there were enough of them to make the place seem like paradise on earth and my mind frequently dwelt on all those lovely girls flitting around from ward to ward, giving us a treat on each appearance. There was a sudden desire to get one's self well, in order to get up and about amongst all these young ladies. To a young lad like myself the prospects seemed boundless and there was always plenty of verbal stimulus from my fellow patients. I suppose its no different to a bunch of young lads at a dance hall, all eyeing the girls on the dance floor.

Their crude remarks were a constant source of amusement, but I bet the physios would never even enter the wards had they known what was in the minds of my fellow patient!

Talk about variety being the spice of life-the physio's were from all parts of the world, namely Germany, Holland, Sweden, Norway, America, Australia, Canada, and of course our own beauties from The United Kingdom. To attend to the practical part of their activities, I should explain that a physio would attend the ward four times a day to treat a new patient. After 4 weeks this was reduced to 3 visits and after six weeks to twice a day. Each therapist had several cases to treat, all at different stages of progress. The oldest of her patients may have been in hospital for eight to twelve months, whilst her other cases were at differing stages of improvement.

The back cases could partially help themselves with treatment, whereas the neck cases were more difficult from the work load point of view, needing more daily attention, especially after having left their beds for a wheelchair. And for this reason a physio would not usually have more than four or five neck cases under her charge at any one time, as she would have been unable to cope.

Consequently, the physio staff were often very hard pressed and received our every sympathy. They had to keep an assortment of muscle and bone joints loosened up; so they had to carry out what are known as ' passive movements ' on limbs, to prevent them from becoming paralysed through inertia. Therefore, a back case would need his legs regularly exercised, whereas a neck case would need both his legs and arms regularly exercised. And the importance of keeping all of the joints well loosened up early on, can not be overstressed, as it is possible at such an early stage that the individual will greatly improve, once any bruising to the cord has later subsided.

Sometimes a physio would consider it useful to use electrical equipment on weak or unresponsive muscles to obtain a stronger response. A weak muscle response could result from an impulse from the brain being impeded on route at the damaged cord area, so an electrical shock might usefully coincide a brain impulse and prompt the muscle back into use. Yet it is imperative to understand that this treatment will only be of positive use where a weak brain impulse is already getting through.

It was standard procedure for all cervical patients to receive bed treatment four times a day, but I didn't immediately realise this. I thought that my particular physio had taken a shine to me because of all the time she was spending on my exercises. Being only seventeen years of age, I was swiftly drawn to this physio even though I knew she was a few years older than myself. Four times a day she came into the ward to see little old me and I couldn't help fancying myself as the original Prince charming. I would lay making plans to date her just as soon as I could be well enough to get up and about.

This beautiful physio just beamed every time she came into the ward and I told myself it just wasn't possible for her to be this way with any other patient. I had it bad; I couldn't get over her and my boyish crush blossomed into overwhelming love. I had learned in very quick time that it could take eighteen months before one would know how permanent a spinal injury might be. This period of time was the limit which one can expect to regain any further movement or feeling, as the nerves below the lesion are then accepted as being obsolete. I should add that the lesion in my case was c5-c6 in my neck, which in non medical terms would be approximately shirt collar height.

I was thinking that our feelings for each other might be mutual and was mindful of the fact that in my current condition, I might not be much of a catch. I had now been at Stoke Mandeville for six weeks and I recall it was a Friday morning when my sweetheart came trotting into the ward. The sheer sight of my physio sent my heart pumping faster and somehow my world was immediately better. To my shock horror she approached my bed only then to explain that she was getting married the next day. I was now feeling shattered and was left completely speechless. My physio then did an about turn and trotted off again.

The next few days were quite difficult for me, because, I suppose the realisation that the physio's were there merely to brighten up our lives, hit me hard. In hindsight, I had completely misread all of the verbal and physical exchanges, that we had enjoyed together. On the third or forth day after learning of her intended marriage, I was informed that she had in fact married a quadriplegic. Well, despite my own feelings of love for her, I was actually pleased to hear that she had married a fellow quadriplegic. In the fullness of time, I further learned that they were very happily married and also had a child together. Sufficient time had now passed, my wounds were now healed, and I was simply delighted for them.

Quite soon after arriving at Stoke Mandeville my lovely mum visited me and brought my favourite sandwiches with her. What a blessing – good old chicken and mayo, I can taste them as I write these words. Mum was a little upset at the sight of me still on the bed with my head calipers and appropriate weights, hanging beyond the headboard. My brothers David and Michael had accompanied mum on the train journey, which they informed me took at best, two hours. Despite my predicament it was lovely to have family at my bedside. My brothers seemed shocked at the degree of damage, that had been caused by my accident.

It was immediately apparent to them, that I had already lost a lot of weight, due to the paralysis. Prior to the accident I had a very good physique, which I had developed during both my swimming training and gymnastics. I told them that the weight loss was inevitable during the first months of treatment and could in fact be helpful with regard to avoiding bed sores. I explained to my mum and brothers that I would probably be kept in traction for a minimum of 3 months.   It was hoped by the doctors that the fractured vertebrae in my neck would heal over the three month period. It was envisaged that the head calipers could then be removed and a small degree of recovery might be forthcoming. Well, before I knew it, the day had passed and my family were saying their goodbyes. It may sound daft, but I was now ready for their departure. I actually loved their company, but was now feeling exhausted. I recall Mum, David and Michael walking the short distance to the wards double doors, where they waved goodbye, with a concerned look on their faces.

Fellow sufferers.

The following morning was quiet on the ward and I was now due for my afternoon bed turn, which resulted in me facing the chap in the bed next to mine. We had previously exchanged a few words, but because we were both rather breathless at the time, it was too difficult for us to speak loudly enough to be heard. Now that the turns were in our favour, we were facing each other and could speak. He had been in hospital two weeks longer than me and also had a set of head traction calipers on his head. He looked very odd with the metal screwed into his head and I found myself laughing at him, asking him at the same time if my head traction looked as grotesque as his. He stated that he thought so and started laughing at mine.

Being in similar circumstances we could readily appreciate each others predicament, so the

more we looked at each other the more we laughed,
causing our head caliper traction to hurt as our
heads shook with laughter. We both had our spirits
lifted by this short period of laughter, which had
verged on being hysterical. As time passed we
became good friends and would talk ' the hind leg
off the donkey '. He was in his thirties and had
sustained his broken neck in a car crash. It
transpired that road traffic accidents caused the
majority of spinal injury, followed by swimming
and sporting accidents. As things stood, I was in
third place, having broken my neck in the
gymnasium ! My new friend was unable to recall
what had happened to him, at the time of the
crash.

I later learned that many of the car crash
victims were unable to recall anything about the
accident, probably because the details were too
horrific, to be recalled to the conscious mind. The
loss of memory was often caused also by severe
injury and trauma to the head. We were both c 5/6
cases and we therefore had similar difficulties to
overcome, when getting up at the conclusion of our
first three months of hospitalisation.

My fellow patient was unluckier than I
because when he was seated in his wheelchair his

rump became persistently too sore to be sat on. He was constantly returned to his bed to relieve his backside pressure. If he remained sitting in his wheelchair for too long a period, his backside could easily have broken out into numerous sores, which could then leave him bedridden for months. He would be turned from side to side to keep his backside, pressure free. Humans of course were designed to stand when necessary, but accidental paralysis removed our ability to stand. It was important to spend short periods of time sitting in the wheelchair, until such time that the backside became accustomed ' to its newly found importance '.

I feel now that we should move on from sores and tell you a little about the hospital itself. It had been built during the war, consisting of a large complex of single storey wooden huts joined together by corridors. Annexes at the end of each ward had originally accommodated military Officers, but now their doors had been fixed back and they were now extensions to the wards.

Beds were allocated so that as new patients came into the intake wards they were placed in beds by the entrance and as they became older inhabitants they were moved up the ward to the far end, into the annex and finally out into the other wards. This constant moving of patients up the ward boosted morale, because one could judge one's medical progress by bed positions. There was an odd feeling at times, as though one was moving into foreign territory among other patients, some of whom were not always compatible. Generally though there was a good atmosphere engendered by common suffering and experience.

Apart from me and my neighbour, there were twenty two other patients in the ward, all with spinal injuries sustained in a variety of accidents. Naturally the longer I was there the more folk I got to know, as everyone would pass the time discussing how each had had his or her accident. We had a good cross section of society in our ward, for fate had chosen its victims indiscriminately. My first neighbour was a Managing Director of an engineering company and beyond him was the Managing Director of a publishing company, who had also broken his neck in a motor vehicle accident. This poor chap had to cope with 16 lbs of weight on his head traction. He was driving home one evening when he was met by a drunken driver who had driven through a red traffic light and collided with his vehicle. As a result of the impact he was thrown out of his car, landing yards away, wrapped around a street lamp post. Such an event is a strong recommendation to the wearing of seat belts, however you may view it.

On the opposite side of the ward there were two young lads and two older men. These stood out in my memory because I progressed up the ward with them. One of the lads, a constant joker, had broken his neck in a car smash, at a slightly lower level of lesion than my own, at C 6/7. The other lad had been involved in a motor-cycle accident and for the first few days in the ward he was completely delirious, causing everyone to laugh at his ravings. He was particularly vociferous at night, always calling out about the night staff trying to kill him. Mercilessly, the whole ward would play along with this idea and stir things up, to the point where he was trying to get out of bed. But, as he had done a good job of breaking his neck, at c6, he was unable to move very far, which was a good thing as it would have been very painful for him to tear his head traction calipers out of his skull.

Whilst overtaking a bus, the bus itself overtook a parked vehicle and he finished up jammed between the front wheel and mudguard of the bus. The lad had to be cut free and had sustained multiple injuries in addition to a broken neck, but he was lucky to have survived at all. Due to his multiple injuries, he had to be nursed on a system known as bed packs. This entailed placing pillows, neck rolls and similar packing under the body with a view to preventing bed sores. After a couple of days the young lad stopped suffering deliriousness and settled back down to a degree of normal neck break recovery. In effect he started to progress along with the rest of us. A few days later, like a bolt out of the blue, his lungs collapsed. The doctors managed to re-inflate his lungs, but it was a close call and the experience shook him up big time. His lung capacity was quite small at the time and this was the main cause of the collapse. He was warned by the doctors to cut down on heavy smoking at the time and wisely, he stopped smoking immediately.

One of the two older men had broken his neck in a pit accident in a Welsh coal mine and the other had broken his back falling off the top of a fire-engine ladder. The minor had probably led a tough energetic life, but as each week passed, he became increasingly depressed over his misfortune. He coughed constantly, night and day and having experienced some of that myself, at a later date, I know what he must have been going through. There were often two physios pounding on his chest simultaneously in an effort to break up his lung congestion. Years of coal dust had accumulated on his chest and the moment the physios got one lot of phlegm up, there was immediately another, causing him to cough violently. Such continuous coughing is extremely strenuous and having to remain flat out in bed for the necessary three months, didn't help him at all.

He was frequently overheard to be praying aloud to God. I suspect everyone else in the ward often did the same thing, but quietly. He was pleading for God to be merciful and to let him off the hook, but his wishes were not granted. Having been a fit miner all his life, his predicament was particularly hard to take and I later learned that between 1947 and 1973 seven and a half thousand men were killed in pit accidents throughout Britain. You might be of the opinion that he was one of the lucky ones, but then, that is a matter for conjecture.

The fireman also found his situation hard to accept, perhaps because he to had led a fit and active life for so long. He was seemingly completely baffled as to why such a nice bloke as himself had been singled out to 'cop it ', and later on, when the time came for him to get up to rehabilitate himself to life in a wheel chair, he just couldn't take it. Although he was physically much better off than those of us who had sustained broken necks, as he still had the use of his arms and hands, he actually felt less fortunate because back break cases were supposed to do everything for them selves, whereas he could see that the neck cases had the 'privilege ' of having practically everything done for them.

He could not reach his feet properly whilst attempting to dress himself, because his legs were just a little bit too long and heavy. Thus, he couldn't quite manage to hold either of his legs bent up long enough to enable him to achieve putting his socks on. Every time he managed to get his leg bent up, he would attempt to put a sock on and forget about the need to support the leg simultaneously, when it would fall down straight again without his having put the sock on his foot. Day after day, he would attempt to put his socks on unsuccessfully, until a passing member of staff would take pity and do the job for him. But each and every day, he would end up crying like a baby first.

Incontinence: Bowels – Bladder.

After a few days in hospital, a new patient is automatically introduced to the delights involved with being incontinent. So, those without normal bowel control have to adjust to the idea that they are to endure a manual bowel evacuation every other day henceforth.

The evening before the bowels were due for clearing, I was given three small yellow tablets to swallow and told by the nurse that I was listed for ' evacuations ' the following morning. When I asked her just what evacuations were all about, she laughed and told me I would learn soon enough. I went off to sleep that night with quite a tummy ache and when I was awoken the following morning at the six o'clock turn time, I had a terrible shock. The bedclothes were pulled back and a ghastly smell hit the air. I had had a bowel action whilst asleep. I was very embarrassed, I just couldn't fathom how it had happened without my awareness.

The sheets and pillows were smothered and the charge nurse mentioned something about the bloody day staff having dished out too strong a laxative, because they knew they wouldn't have to clear it up. The orderlies lowered the bed down to the flat position and then turned me onto my side. This was standard procedure for those having their bowels sorted out and each morning they had to remain on their sides for the following four hours until being turned again at ten by the day staff. The charge nurse told me that although I had had a first rate result it was still necessary for me to be placed onto my side, because I was on the evacuation list. He then sarcastically pointed out that if I was not in the correct position when the day staff sister came on duty, she would kick up a fuss about the night staffs inefficiency. I decided that ' sarcasm was certainly the lowest form of wit ' in all the circumstances faced by me that morning. I also decided that I would let things like this roll of my back-for want of a better word of course!!

Whenever one is down on the evacuation list for the following day, the day staff usually ensure that a number of incontinence sheets are suitably positioned in case an over strong laxative causes an early bowel motion. Clearly someone had got it wrong with me on this particular day, but hey, who cares. Worst things happen at sea! All my bed linen had to be changed and this was the first occasion on which I sincerely cursed the night staff, as they rolled me from side to side in a rough manner in what I assumed to be some form of protest, at having to both clean me up and change the bed.

However, such rough treatment turned out to be rather commonplace whenever I had to be manually turned over onto my side without the use of the turning bed and all the patients agreed that it was unnecessary for us to be handled so roughly, particularly whilst patients were still on head traction. Evacuations were carried out on alternative days without fail. After an evacuation had been completed was the happiest time of a two day period, but as the hours dwindled away, the grim prospect of being turned on one's side again was quite unpleasant to contemplate.

Although bowel incontinence can be very troublesome for a new case, it should not be allowed to be the dominating factor in one's life immediately after the completion of the three months in bed and after one has been discharged. The ' fear' that can develop from one's constantly having irregular bowel actions whilst up and dressed can create a very morbid attitude as to the future; but, in time, using a personally correct aperient, coupled with not eating anything after having taken it, the bowel difficulties can be overcome.

I hope I'm not dragging everyone down during this chapter, but I feel it very important that people in general are made aware of the many health complications suffered by both paraplegics and quadriplegics. What can one say about the medical staff, other than the fact that they are all Angels. The challenges faced by both us and them each day are simply enormous and this is why I occasionally go into great detail. Please bear with me and I will assure you of one thing, your knowledge of a great hospital and it's day to day patients will expand enormously.

The majority of cervical cases have to use suppositories to cause a bowel motion and it is frequently the case that a residual mixture of excreta and suppository can be left in the bowel after the evacuation is complete. Therefore, it is a wise cervical ' indeed ' who gets a third party to check manually inside the bowel an hour or so after evacuation and of course prior to being dressed. This of course allows one to get up with renewed confidence, in the knowledge that ' there will be no residual. An action every other day is the ideal, but if your off on a trip for a few days, or going out early on a supposed evacuation morning, then you can always leave the bowel alone for three or four days, before having them cleared out again. Let's now move onto a more interesting subject, yes you've guessed it – the bladder.

The Bladder.

Generally speaking if a patient has become incontinent in the bowels, then the bladder will also be affected. When a fit person wishes to pass water, he or she sends a message from the brain to a muscle in the bladder called the sphincter and this muscle moves to one side to allow one to pass urine. If you are paralysed, however, the muscle receives no such message, so the bladder continues to blow up and when too full, the urine may be forced back up into the kidneys, resulting in kidney infection from the bacteria in the water. Therefore, to prevent this from happening and to start one off with bladder training, one's bladder is emptied manually for the first week or two of hospitalisation. Emptying is accomplished by a plastic or rubber tube called a catheter being passed into the bladder to drain the urine off. When empty the catheter is withdrawn and the bladder refills ready for the next drainage time. The bladder training would continue into one's second week in the hospital, until the bladder eventually developed an automatic contraction reaction when full; forcing the urine out via the urethral canal, without the necessity of a catheter having to be introduced. This was the required aim of the entire bladder training programme, when catheterising could cease.

At this stage of bladder training most of the men could begin wearing condom sheaths. These are similar to ordinary prophylactics, but more durable. They are attached by means of an adhesive, to enable us to keep reasonably dry. Actually being glued up around one's private parts is unpleasant at first, but in order to keep dry – inevitable. I was averse to the idea of having to wear such a device for a full twenty four hours a day and thus, whenever I was put to bed I had it taken off and replaced by a bed bottle. This duly proved to be inadequate as developing involuntary muscle spasms throughout my body, caused me to be thrown rather violently away from the bottle, when

the bed needed changing several times a night. A
new case will save himself much suffering if he
accepts the full time wearing of a sheath, from the
word go. At night, the condom is connected up to a
night drainage bag, or bottle and during the day it
is connected up to a urinal tied to one's leg, which,
when full, can be emptied virtually anywhere by
means of releasing a small tap at the lower end of
the bag.

Understaffed orderlies are constantly pushed
for time and they consequently tend to put
condoms on hurriedly, causing leaking later on.
New patients tend to become very depressed as to
the wearing of condoms in future, assuming that
they are forever going to get wet when fully dressed
as a result of leaky condoms. There is definitely a
right and a wrong way to the condom changing
procedure, which, does not become apparent to the
new patients until they have suffered many, many
months of getting wet when dressed.

Suffering can be largely avoided if the new
patient keeps an eye on the person changing the
condom, to ensure that a leak proof job is carried
out. The old condom should be taken off with
some care, in order to avoid any undue tearing of
the skin area and if possible, an erection should be

cultivated, as this makes it much easier for the changer to handle the penis. The new condom should be heard and seen to be pierced, to allow a free flow of water; it should be partially unrolled to one third down over the penis, and the remaining two thirds of skin area should be liberally covered in adhesive. When tacky, the condom can be fully rolled down and when dry the wearer concerned should have no problems for the following forty eight hours. If a lesser area of adhesive is attempted the condom will probably come off and if a greater area the condom will very likely glue itself together and later burst.

Not all men can wear a condom sheath successfully, for some have a greasy skin to which the latex solution will not adhere, when the condom leaks or persistently comes off. Others discover that their bladder cannot be trained to contract when full and it is then necessary for such people to have a permanently indwelling catheter instead of an external condom, as this is the only means by which their water can be successfully drained from the bladder. The catheter has to be changed every six weeks or so, when all the necessary equipment has to be thoroughly sterilised. The wearer is open to infection as the inside of the tube allows germs in the drainage bag to get back into the bladder. With a condom, however, the urethral passage closes once one has passed and this cuts down the likelihood of one's contracting any such infection.

Ideally, one's water should be mainly acid, such acidity helping to prevent the spread of any bacteria present in the water and helping prevent the formation of any stones in bladder or kidneys. A pill known as a G500 helps provide such acidity. They were provided four at a time, four times a day, seven days a week, with a backlog causing one to have to swallow perhaps twelve at a time. It was claimed that we were to take these pills for the rest of our life, but I have since been able to cut them out altogether and experience no adverse effect, so far.

Although, different means are now used for gaining such acidity, the female incontinence is a far greater problem, since the incontinence cannot be controlled by the wearing of a condom urinal. Some have to have indwelling catheters and the remainder have to go to the lavatory several times a day and express the urine from the bladder, before the bladder becomes full and an automatic contraction occurs. They do have to ensure that an accessible toilet is available wherever they might be, but practice makes perfect and eventually they learn how to remain quite dry.

As with the incontinent bowels, so it is with one's incontinent bladder; neither should be allowed to rule one's life when up and dressed and an alert individual will see to it, that they do not.

A typical ward day.

In a way, the days of hospital ward life were not separate, as no sooner had the 10p.m. turn been completed than the following day's 2 am. turn had arrived. Then a little sleep was snatched before everyone was duly roused by the orderlies preparing for the 6 am. turns and early morning tea. Half the patients were down for evacuations and if it happened to be your day you were duly turned onto your side and given the customary knock, twist, or pull on the traction during the process. Oh and a couple of suppositories were hastily administered.

The charge nurse would have dished out the pills, when one would frequently end up in the ludicrous situation of having one orderly doing a manual evacuation at one end, whilst another was administering pills and tea at the other. The conditions for enjoying a nice cup of tea were far from perfect, as I'm sure you can imagine.

At 8am the day shift orderlies would wash all the cervical patients, before giving them their cold breakfast, which had been dished up too early by the nursing staff. Then at 10am the next turns were carried out, when anyone who had been left dirty by the night staff would finally be cleaned up.

The staff were then sent off for their coffee break and the cervical cases would be given cold coffee upon their return. If unlucky, the day sister would then remember that it was your day to have your head traction dressings changed. A nurse would then drive one to the edge of insanity with her attempting to do a quick shaving job on one's scalp. Blood and lymph had oozed out of the scull holes and set hard and the nurse would merrily tear at the tender skin, bunging the safety razor up further still, as she went. Patients on head traction were distraught, anyway and with a relentless attack on one's head wounds taking place, the needless pain was enough to make a good man break down and cry. Believe me when I say it was a relief when she had finished this particular, 'act of care'!

Lunch time arrived at twelve and again the cervical's meals were served well in advance of there being enough staff free to attend to feeding. Then, if it was cleaning day, a chap would dress the floor with a polish which caused all of the patients to feel sick. At 2pm we were all turned again and given another cold cup of tea at three.

If not being fed, turned, or tortured, there were one or two things to be done to help pass the time, but the more severely paralysed one was, the less there was to do. The television could be watched ... if one happened to be facing in that direction, but the small screen presented a strain to one's eyes and the volume had to be minimal as many of the patients were often feeling rough. However the volume problem was remedied with the installation of an earphone system, which could also be channelled into radio programmes.

The severely paralysed were paralysed in the arms and hands to varying extents and therefore a book or newspaper could not be readily ' held '. To overcome this, the occupational therapy staff supplied prismatic glasses, which, enabled someone lying flat on their back to read a book or newspaper propped up on a stand a little way down the bed. This could be frustrating as one continually had to catch the attention of a third party to turn the next page. The glasses worked on the same principle of reflecting mirrors as that used in a periscope and although they were a strain on the eyes they did help overcome some of the boredom.

An alternative to the prismatic glasses, there was another form of amusement known as the ' talking book'. A library of thrillers and the like, which had been read onto tape. A cervical could just lay back and listen on some earphones and the tape tracks had to be switched every two hours by the staff; so it was less troublesome than the glasses and book set up. The two tape machines were in big demand and it amazes me now as to just how many books I listened to. These tapes were none other than a ' God send ' for patients as badly injured as I!! Without these talking books, life could be unbearable, but now we had a means of escape, from the day to day boredom.

The back cases were capable of some occupational therapy whilst bed bound, such as the likes of basket making or weaving; and the cervical cases were encouraged to exercise their arms wherever possible, by an occupational therapist aiding them with the beginnings of a small handbag, which was later attached to one's wheelchair. Although, I now recall, that very early on I began this therapy using my teeth to grip the weaving strands.

When the nursing staff returned from tea they would do some of the wound dressings and the orderlies would do some bed-baths. At six the meal would be rushed through and the turns would be carried out. At eight the night staff returned and after the 10pm. turn we would all settle down to await the following day's 2am. turn, once again.

Some significant progress;
and an embarrassment.

After approximately six weeks in hospital, I began to develop some movement in my arms, as the bruising to my spinal cord lesion improved. Seeing this, my physio made good use of the electrical impulse equipment to stimulate my wrists pull back muscles into a stronger response. I could now move my deltoid shoulder muscles, my bicep arm muscles and my wrist extensor muscles. My physio was eventually able to regrade my lesion level to that of a low c 5/6 incomplete sensory, complete motor power. Although this downgrading did not provide me with control of the very important tricep muscles, at the back of the upper arm, as these muscles do not become controllable until we drop down to level c6/7.

However, my improvement was very important, as control of the pull back wrists muscles later enable one to perfect the art of manipulating light objects with one's paralysed hands. At level c5, or higher, this cannot be done.

My right arm being stronger, I could readily bring my hand to my mouth and I accordingly experimented by one day asking an orderly to place an apple between my palm and teeth. It was difficult to eat, as I was chuckling whilst chewing and holding it against my mouth with the weight of my hand. But, it was very enjoyable, even though I eventually had to lay a while before someone removed the wet core I later dropped down my neck.

With my new grading I was left in quite a dilemma, as I didn't know whether or not I would continue to improve in the weeks to come. I also had concerns as to how I would improve after getting up from a rather long period of my life, lying in bed; bed not being perhaps the best description of the first six weeks. The improvement issue was particularly perplexing because there was a young man from the far end of the ward who had been declared to be a similar level lesion injury to me, who pushed his wheelchair up and down the ward, inch by inch, in a very pathetic manner and there was also a middle aged man, a stockbroker, who was not only up and walking about, but gleefully claimed that this was the second time that he had broken his neck, at c5/6.

The million dollar question was, will I be up soon walking about, as was the stockbroker or would I spend the rest of my life in a wheelchair, pushing it around at the same pace as the earlier

mentioned young man?

At the time I was completely ignorant of hairline fractures, or complete or incomplete lesions and that's why I was so baffled. In fact the young man had broken his neck at c5/6 and had made a good job of it apparently, as I had done. The stockbroker had also broken his neck at this level, except he had only suffered a hairline fracture and

he hadn't sustained any permanent degree of
paralysis. He must have been one of the luckiest
men on earth to have come out of spinal injury
twice, unscathed. I must admit that a slight feeling
of ' sour grapes ' could easily set in, if one was to
dwell too long on this particular ' gentleman '.

The staff never actually told a patient
whether or not he or she was going to be paralysed
for life and the patients never discussed it at length
amongst them selves. So, after much consideration,
I decided against putting the question to my physio
... just in case she dashed my hopes and told me I
was going to be the same as the unfortunate young
man up the ward.

The other patients informed me that the
doctors usually left the head traction in place for
five or six weeks- depending on the state of the
fracture and I had therefore begun to nag them
about taking mine off shortly after my fifth week,
but, each time I asked, I was told no, as the break
hadn't healed sufficiently. On reaching the six
week mark I began to suspect the doctors of
conspiring against me, to make me suffer as long as
possible, with the caliper knocks and head dressing
changes. I perhaps should explain that the head
caliper knocks came about when moved into

different positions by the nurses, to prevent bed sores occurring.

Seven and eight weeks had now passed, with my persistently receiving a negative reply to my pleading. Then half way through my ninth week a consultant walked up to my bed and nonchalantly declared I could have the calipers removed that very minute ... and I had just been through hell again, having the dressings changed. Without further ado he released a spring mechanism at the top of the calipers and they sprung out of my skull, tearing the dressings off as they came away. I winced at the pain and I was momentarily unsure as to whether I was happy with them off as I felt as though my head was floating up in the air, as my legs had felt, way back when my accident occurred.

In truth it was one of the most enjoyable moments of my young life, to have been relieved of wearing those damned calipers. Yet, I was emotionally attached to them, so I asked the doctor if I could keep them as a memento; but to my disappointment he said no, explaining that they were an expensive piece of precision engineering, which would have to be returned to hackney hospital, in readiness for any knew patient that they might receive. The thought God help him, sprung to mind.

My head wounds were then redressed on several subsequent occasions without the necessity of the hair being shaved off ... the word 'Alleluia' now seemed appropriate!! It took a few more months for the skull holes to heal properly. With a clock face in mind, I could now turn my head to 9am. on my left side and 3 pm. on my right. This may seem to be a small consideration, but believe it or not, it was bloody marvellous! When the traction had been in place, the thought would often be, will I be able to move my head – as described? Well folks, I now had the answer.

With the head traction gone, all I had to do was lie back and relax for the following three weeks, prior to being given the green light to get up.

An embarrassment.

Shortly after my tenth week I was quietly listening to my talking book one afternoon, when I noticed a whole troop of young ladies entering the ward. I watched them with a certain amount of interest, as there were a few very attractive girls amongst their number; when to my delight, they were gathered together around my bed. The doctor removed my earphones and when asked for my permission to be used for demonstration purposes, I unwittingly consented. You may recall my embarrassment at Hackney hospital, when the nurses took my shorts off, but now I hadn't the slightest inkling, as to what I had let myself in for. The doctor stripped me completely of my bedclothes and there I was for all the world (plus twenty odd girls) to see, in my birthday suit, yet again. To make matters worse, a newly fitted condom had caused the development of an erection.

For the next twenty minutes the doctor was cheerfully pointing out where I could or couldn't feel, or where I could or couldn't move, when all the time I didn't know where to hide my face. I had never been so embarrassed in my entire life, but one thing is for sure and that is that I have never become embarrassed due to this uncontrollable bodily reaction, ever since.

I mentioned this incident, however, solely because it raises the moral question as to whether hospital in-patients generally should be used for demonstration purposes for the trainee nurses and doctors.

Admittedly, I had granted my permission, but I had been unaware that this granted the doctor the licence to strip me of my bedclothes. Yet, apparently, this practice is a common occurrence throughout all British teaching hospitals. Thus, I contend that there is a good case for a patient being informed 'beforehand' just what he is letting himself in for, before he grants permission. At the time of writing, there is a bill passing through Parliament to legislate against this practice of using patients for demonstration purposes. I'm sorry if it appears that I have gone a little deep, with this aspect of hospitalisation! I suppose there are good arguments on both sides with regard to this question.

Getting up; Dressing.

The end of my twelfth week arrived and I was given the all clear for being gotten up, although, I had no idea what a difficult business this was going to be. Apart from paralysis, I had become extremely weak, making it necessary to be weaned out of bed very gradually, by being sat up at increasingly higher angles each day. Even being raised to an angle of fifteen degrees made one become giddy, as the shallow breathing and poor circulation did not allow sufficient oxygen to be taken into the system. I'm afraid the thought going through your mind was not one of happy days!!

On the fourth or fifth day, I was raised to an angle of sixty degrees or so, when I experienced just what it meant to be unable to control the movements of one's trunk. The pillows had been incorrectly positioned at my back and I realised that I was gradually slipping over towards the floor. I couldn't even correct myself with my arms, as I was unable to push against them from the elbows, having no tricep control. Fortunately a member of staff came to my rescue and sat me up squarely again. This of course was a yet another blow to my pride!

The higher one was sat up, the more the stomach tended to bulge, as the stomach muscles had relaxed to a considerable extent. And, therefore, one's diaphragm would drop lower as the intestines were not actually providing any active support, causing breathing to become yet shallower, with a consequential lower oxygen intake.

Generally, the higher the level of injury the longer one would take to be able to sit fully upright, but a few days to a week was usually sufficient. At this stage one could progress to being sat up in a wheelchair for a few minutes, with one's legs straight out on a stool or chair, in order to put not too great a strain on the circulation straight off.

If giddiness was experienced, the legs would be raised and the wheelchair tipped backwards to ease the circulation; but, as this is frequently insufficient a remedy for higher lesion cervical' s, they often have to be completely laid out on the bed. When such a situation occurs, a cervical often passes out before he is able to call out and having been left sitting in an unconscious state myself, on many occasions, I can testify as to what an unpleasant experience it can be. It is very important to keep an eye on cervical patients who are experiencing this sitting up phase, as if they are left in the chair unconscious it can set them back a week or so and can also cause slurred speech for a day or two.

Passing out is preceded by a buzzing in the ears and clouding over of the eyes, so if one experiences this when a member of staff or one 's physio is not present, call out for help immediately. Should a high neck case continually pass out at each attempt to wean him into a wheelchair, it may be that he is in need of some form of artificial stomach support to help support the diaphragm. Such a support is worn in the form of a criss-crossing cloth body-belt, which is wrapped around one's waist prior to being dressed and lifted into the chair. The belt allows one to breath sufficiently deeply as the diaphragm is supported.

I had to make use of such a body-belt on several occasions, after having had to spend varying amounts of time in bed, but, eventually, I was able to be gotten straight up after several weeks in bed without the necessity of resorting to the belt.

Dressing.

After a week to ten days, however, a patient should have reached the stage whereby the ward sister will give him the go ahead to be gotten up and actually dressed, when one really feels as if he is making some significant progress.

On the whole, most orderlies didn't much care as to how well one was dressed, just as long as that was another patient, up and dressed for that day. One's pride had definitely had to go as a result of one's fall. Socks were put on back to front or inside out; trousers were left half way down one's backside, with the legs twisted everywhere, looking all the worse because they were often found to be too tight in the leg that had to have the urine drainage bag tied to it; your shirt would be left hanging out, where it would remain as you couldn't tuck it in without any grip in the hands and your pullover was never, ever, put on nice and squarely.

Having been dressed, you were placed in the wheelchair and sat at every angle excepting an upright one, causing you to fall all over the place, because you couldn't balance yourself. This prevented you from doing anything constructive, such as feeding or washing yourself, even had you perhaps been capable of achieving this in the first place. I don't wish to sound like a depressed individual, but when suffering severe paralysis, all of these matters are so very important in helping us build our confidence.

There are a thousand and one ways in which one can become wet when up, that are not even remotely suspected by a new patient, until he has had several years experience of avoiding them. The point of dressing, if you're a cervical, is the time to be alert. The back cases are alright, as if they have a mishap, that's there own fault. Most males wear condoms which should be thoroughly stuck on and well sealed with the appropriate glue. The condom must be well holed at the connection and water tight ! It should never be too tightly stretched, twisted, or doubled up. The tubing must be thoroughly pressed onto the top of the urine bag and the urine bag screw top must be tightly screwed home. The bag needed to be flat against the inside of the leg, just below the knee and the tap at the lower end should be turned off.

The trousers should be loose, or even a few sizes too big; since tight trousers can cause the waterworks to cease flowing and burst the condom. A third party should always have the pleasure of checking on your pants, when your seated in the chair, to ensure they are not squashing the scrotum or cutting off the free flow of water in the condom.

Even though one cannot feel any physical discomfort when wet, there is definitely a psychological effect in thinking, "Oh, I've wet my bloody self again, which can be sole destroying in the extreme, when it happens daily, weekly, and monthly, every single day.

When all the above points were carried out with due care and proper consideration, cervical patients day to day lives, benefited enormously!

The test, as to whether my explanations are too detailed in this particular arena, would be for the average reader to sit in a chair, fully dressed and urinate. I'm sure all participants would find the test a very unpleasant experience, indeed. Not all cervical patients are bitter and twisted, but we feel that despite the good work of the hospital staff, there was always room for improvement.

A Sweater?

For the first week, or so, after having been allowed up, cervicals have to wear a stiff plastic collar support, in order to ensure against any inadvertent head movements causing damage to the newly healed fracture. The back lesion cases have to wear stiff plastic corsets, which look very much like breast plate armour and perhaps not surprisingly, with all this stiffness, any movements made by either cervical or back case had a very odd mechanical look about them.

For reasons not understood by the doctors, some cases were in a constant state of sweating and more so with cervical cases. Only about one case in twenty turned out to be a sweater and when I say sweating, I know what I'm talking about, because I was unlucky enough to be one of the chosen few.

It was more profuse when up and dressed and some of the doctors believe it is a symptom caused by psychological stress from one's new found situation, but, I think this is a wrong assumption. After only an hour or two in the chair one's upper clothes would be completely soaked through, this being due to the fact that it was only the non paralysed skin areas which produced all the sweat.

In my case, the head and shoulders and upper arms... but not the armpits. It never ceased oozing out and it was a constant annoyance to have it perpetually dripping off of one's nose and chin. When the plastic collar was being worn, any runs down the inside would cause one to shudder as they couldn't be got at with a towel.

If you could sit still it wasn't too uncomfortable, but this was not on, because the ward sister would always be telling you to 'move yourself ' off to the classes that had to be attended elsewhere in the hospital. Then, as a breeze seemed to increase extreme tenseness around the neck and shoulders, this would have to be suffered, as all the corridor windows were always wide open. The clothes became wetter and the shivers would set in as the clothes became more clammy.

When my collar had been discarded, after about two weeks, I took to carrying a towel around for mopping up operations, which did make life a little less uncomfortable, although the sweating never eased up.

I later met a chap, a Liverpudlian, who had had the same problem, some twelve years previously, who informed me it had been two years before his sweating had ceased...thus making me feel terrible at the thoughts of having to endure it for a full two years, yet, oddly enough, that was just how long it did take to stop. At the time, it developed into a great source of self pity as to why poor old me had had to be singled out to be a sweat case... and as no one could explain why one was or was not a sweater, I and numerous others were forever trying to figure out the causes.

It was generally agreed that it was caused by all the pressure building up whilst one was up and dressed. There was backside and back pressure building up due to the lack of circulation to those areas; bowel and bladder pressure due to these being frequently full and stomach and leg pressure caused by the urinal strapping supports.

I hope I'm not boring you with this aspect of paralysis, but for the sufferers of, I feel it worthy of a detailed account. We were all aware of these sources of pressure and were aware that we were all subject to them, but, some of us were sweaters and others were not. We just couldn't account for the difference in body reaction and I've no doubt the doctors are still playing around with their theories, as to the causes of our perspiration.

Moving on for a moment, during my second year, one of the lads introduced me to a method of emptying the bladder before it became too full, by knocking it with my hand, known as expressing. But, the problem was that you never knew how full the bladder was at any given time and you would end up banging it when there was nothing there to be expressed. Though I eventually found that banging every hour or so did stem the sweating a little.

With this partial success I set about relieving the body pressure elsewhere, by loosening the urinal support straps, or having the bag, or ' kipper ', as it was known, emptied more frequently before it became too heavy when full. On occasions these measures caused the urine bag to pull the unsupported condom off. Amongst the orderlies, one would then be described as a nuisance!! In more modern times I suppose you would be referred to as ' wet wet wet '. However I'm sure the now well known pop group would not appreciate this.

Other than expressing the bladder I never discovered any other worthwhile means of reducing the pressure build- ups, so I decided to sit around the corridors with a towel hunched up around my neck, to await my two years to pass! By doing this of course time passed very slowly.

Everyday chores.

A back case is able to carry out his or her daily washing and grooming chores without too much difficulty and a low lesion neck case with tricep muscle arm control, should also be able to accomplish this, though, with more difficulty.

A case at my level, 5/6, will eventually be able to accomplish shaving, washing, brushing

teeth and combing hair, although, being without
any tricep muscle control makes these tasks rather
difficult to do at first and one may be in need of a
few aides to begin with. At any higher level, c5 or
above, thee tasks cannot usually be accomplished.

These chores may sound like childishly
simple things to have to be overcome but if one
remembers that a cervical has no grip in the hands
the situation can be compared to that of a fit
person attempting to carry out these trifles using a
boxing glove without any thumbs. Further, a low
lesion neck case can hold himself up due to his
tricep control, whereas a cervical without tricep
control cannot support his trunk unless his elbows
are delicately balanced on his chair or armrests or
an arm is hooked behind a chair backrest handle.

Lose balance for a second when your elbow
slips or forget to keep an arm hooked behind the
backrest handle and you end up face down on your
knees. Some cases can sit themselves up again but
some cannot. I personally never managed to be
able to get myself back upright again, consequently
having to stay put until someone came along to sit
me up.

A safety or cut throat razor could not be used
for shaving as they could not be held, therefore an

electric shaver was the answer although there is a problem with 'holding' one in a paralysed hand. A person without triceps will probably need a leather case to be sewn around the razor. This is normally sorted out by someone from the Occupational Therapy Department. A couple of elastic straps are sewn in and this allows the hand to be fitted into them. Then with the razor on the hand all you have to do is learn to shave once more without constantly losing balance and toppling over onto your knees or over the side of the wheelchair armrests. However, pathetic as it may seem you should eventually be able to cup the shaver in your hands and complete a reasonable shave without use of the holder and without perpetually falling onto your knees.

With triceps you should be able to brush your teeth without assistance. A strap with a Velcro fastening is fitted around the palm of the hand to take the toothbrush. At first you may need someone to dispense the paste onto the brush and to oblige with a glass of water for rinsing the mouth out. With practice, the strap can be removed and you can eventually adopt some means of rinsing your mouth out, perhaps via a straw under the tap method.

Washing should be easy for someone with triceps as they can readily put both arms over the sink to squeeze a flannel out or to put some soap on it, whereas very few cervical without triceps can manage to do this as they will be using one arm as a support behind the chair handle. Thus, the problem, how to lather and squeeze a flannel out with only one paralysed hand? The answer lies in not putting the plug in. Run the water onto the soap and flannel, lather the flannel, squeeze it against the side of the basin and bring it out draped over the back of the hand to wash with. The ears and the back of the neck can present a few problems but it does come with practice. You may drop the wet flannel down your neck a few times but do eventually get the hang of it.

Grooming the hair can be extremely trying and until I once grew my hair long I didn't appreciate just how difficult it must be for female cervicals to maintain their long hair. Some male cervicals will not bother with attempting to comb their hair at all but a female cervical will want her house looking good more so now that she is chairbound.

Well, washing a cervicals hair is normally carried out by a third party but with patience any case of c5/6 or lower should be able to manage to comb their hair. A comb cannot be held, therefore a Brush is the answer. A brush with a loop at the back will enable a cervical with triceps to hook his thumb through and for those without the loop should be replaced with a hand strap to enable the fingers to be pushed through it.

Feeding and Drinking.

Feeding can be a problem for a majority of cervicals and from the outset they will probably need to use a palm strap to hold a utensil. Cases of c5 and c4/5 make use of arm and wrist splints to enable them to feed themselves but cases above these levels need to be fed. Whether one has tricep muscle control or not, balance has to been maintained thus leaving only one arm free for feeding.

So, the question is, how does one use a knife and fork? The answer to this is that you can only use a fork or in the case of a real beginner, a spoon. The food has to be cut up by a third party before one can start in on the ensuing fun and games.

At this early stage, cases with tricep control will have weak wrist muscles due to their not having been used regularly for some time. Cases without will also have weak wrist muscles for the same reason and because of the more severe paralysis in the arms. Both will experience difficulty with feeding as they will not be able to gain the necessary high angle of wrist extension for scooping the food onto the spoon or fork.

After a number of mouthfuls have been eaten the wrist muscles will become fatigued, to the extent that the wrist will collapse under the weight of the hand and utensil, resulting in the cervicals being unable to scoop up any more food.

Eventually, sickened by the whole situation, the food which has now been pushed several times around the plate will be pushed off onto the table. Then, still being hungry, many a grown man or woman can be seen resorting to a well tried method of retrieving ones food, namely that of getting your head down to suck the food up straight off of the table. Sounds gross but if you are hungry and nobody is around to help, what else can you do.

I did this on many occasions. From time to time many of my friends thought that I had resorted to this method of feeding. It was in fact the case that I had forgotten about maintaining balance with an arm hooked behind the chair handle and I had fallen face down into my meal. As you may have guessed, whenever this happened (to myself in particular), the air turned very blue.

Finally, when a cervical becomes convinced that they would rather starve than continually have to get their head down to suck the food off of the table, they can be consoled in the knowledge that there exists an item known as a plate guard, a semi circular piece of plastic or perspex, which can be clipped onto the edge of the plate to at as a safety net to prevent the food from continually being pushed onto the table. The food can then be pushed up against the guard and onto the spoon or fork to enable them to eat some of the much needed sustenance before it becomes stone cold.

Try holding 'a hot cup of tea' with a paralysed hand. There is no grip in the fingers for holding the handle and therefore, you have to wait for the tea to become cool before attempting to pick the cup up from its outside wall. The cocking of the wrist method is used, as once you have carefully positioned the fingers and thumb around the cup the pulling back of the wrist causes the finger and thumb tendons to tighten around the cup. The cup can then be carefully lifted up to the mouth, although, not having any feeling in the hands, the cup frequently slips out of your hand and the tea and cup land in your lap. Just as well you can't feel it.

At this early stage however, your wrist will already be worn out after feeding yourself and the cup cannot be picked up by this method until several months later when the wrist muscles have developed a little more. Personally, I dislike cold tea, so I adopted a method of getting my head down to the cup to sip half a cup f tea whilst it was hot, but then the cup would often overbalance and I would be wearing the rest of the tea.

Someone might well conclude that I should have used my other arm for picking the cup up as it was not worn out when feeding, but this could not be done as the fact is that a cervical case usually ends up with one arm being more severely incapacitated than the other. Having almost certainly used the good arm for feeding, the support arm would be of very limited use.

An insulated mug is the ideal container for cervicals to drink out of as this cuts out any risk of burning your hand when attempting to pick up a hot cup of tea and you can pick it up very easily by hooking a thumb through the large handle. Although you cannot carry your personal mug around everywhere you visit I have been amazed as to how many public places have such mugs available for all to use.

A first rate method of increasing the pull back power in your wrist muscles is by practicing the lifting of beer mugs, full ones of course. They have a large handle through which your thumb can be hooked and it is truly amazing how quickly you can cultivate the knack of lifting the glass of beer up to your lips without spilling a single drop. A novice should begin with halves and work up to pints, remembering that regular training is essential for you to develop a 'taste' for these gruelling exercises.

Though, don't be caught out by the fact that it is easier to pick up a mug full of beer than an oddly shaped tea cup. The weight of a pint counterbalances the pull back effect in the wrist and the whole remains steady, but with a cup the wrist wobbles and you can easily drop the cup of tea.

Eventually though, you become an expert, when a cup of tea can be picked up in a public place without it being obvious as to the extent of the paralysis on your hands. Incidentally, concerning the hospitals recommendation that you should drink six pints of fluid a day, apart from tea and coffee etc....some chaps immediately decide to get this volume down them at the local pub....I'm all for them, but they should always ensure that their waterworks are not likely to spring a leak before they set out. It can be extremely embarrassing to have a trail of urine being left behind in public.

Getting about on wheels.

It was good to be getting about the hospital at last, having been trapped in a ward for over three months. The main entrance of the spinal unit brought you into a corridor consisting of administrative offices after which the corridor descended down hill to the public canteen. At the top of the corridor, all the spinal injury wards led off to the left and right, followed at the top by the Stoke Mandeville burns unit wards, which were famous in their own right.

A Split Second Accident

The trip down to the canteen was rather precarious for cervical cases such as I, who couldn't control their chairs sufficiently, as they would just have to let them go careering down hill, along the corridor in the hope of a safe landing at the required destination. It was certainly easier going down than coming up and it took over a year before I could get back up the hills, under my own steam, though this may have been due to the lack of practice arising from the fact that I and numerous other cervicals found it more enjoyable to cadge a lift back up from an unsuspecting young lady.

Alas, these pleasures were few and far between, but a cervical patient had to do... what a cervical patient had to do. These occasional encounters, certainly lifted the spirits of a young man who could well be paralysed for life!

These particular corridors had a gradient of about one in eight and rumour had it that the doctor who pioneered the spinal unit, namely Dr. Guttman, thought them a great source of exercise for his paraplegics. But, of course, those paraplegics could use their hands to propel their chairs and it wasn't until more recent times, when the unit was dealing ever more frequently with quadriplegics, who couldn't use their hands, that those hills caused many a cervical case to curse them.

The wheel rims could not be gripped and to this end the cervical cases are each provided with a leather pair of pushing gloves for exerting their pushing efforts directly onto the tyres. Though, they were not originally glove, but a leather palm covering fastened at the back with Velcro and they had a hole for your thumb to fit through. When going down hill a glove could be held against a tyre or chair wheel rim in order to steer it left or right, but not having feeling in the hands could often result in sustaining mild burns through the gloves, or the glove being pulled off on a spinning wheel and one's hands being cut to pieces.

I had great difficulty in getting these gloves on and the physio suggested that I should hold the glove in my teeth whilst wriggling my thumb through the hole and fastening the Velcro at the back. Although this idea was repugnant at first, I soon got used to it and I was eventually able to get them on without getting too much dirt on my teeth and face, off the gloves.

Although the paraplegics could not propel their chairs much faster than the quadriplegics, it was a case of the quadriplegics being more dangerous as they couldn't stop their chairs very quickly. The consensus of opinion was that the hospital was there for the paralysed and not the fit, so they had better move a bit smartly whenever a wheelchair came careering down the hills, as a footplate smashing into someone's ankles could be very painful indeed. There were often red faces whenever a senior member of the physio department ' caught one at it ' so to speak.

At the bottom of the main corridor was a junction crossing over another corridor, belonging to the general hospital side, which led into the' lower physio ' department. This was the site of many a collision, due to the fact that chairs failed to stop at this junction, before crossing over to the physio department. This was frequently spectacular when an individual was catapulted out of their chair or when someone crashed into a train of the hospital's meal trolley.

The entrance to the canteen was a third of the way down the bottom section of the hills, so it was particularly difficult to steer your wheelchair into it, at a safe speed for the ' docile public ' coming out. Being a c5/6, I could get into the canteen entrance by two methods – either by pushing my right brake on at the precise moment, or by dragging my right arm along the wall to swing the chair around as I came to the entrance. Both methods were in effect too fast for the unsuspecting public, so I later took to cultivating a war cry to alert the public, whenever I was negotiating the entrance corner.

Inside the canteen, a newcomer is presented with rather a sight in the form of a queue consisting of a few people standing up amidst numerous wheelchair customers. The back cases, or even the lower neck cases can manage quite adequately, but, cases without triceps can be presented with some fun and games if they happen to be on their own or with others of a similar level lesion.

Being new, their wallets have to be taken out and the change replaced and the goodies have to be transferred to the table for them. A cream bun and a coffee would have been bought and they would then drop the cream and coffee into their lap. I always had my goodies placed at a table with someone already seated there, as if in luck, a conversation with a young lady could always be started with 'excuse me, could you help me with my coffee, please'. This could be followed by a push up the hills to the wards, by the same unsuspecting young lady. Life was brightening up a little by this time, despite the fact that spring had long since passed. A man and boy may have suffered a broken neck, I was now most probably paralysed for life, but I still had the privilege of young ladies around me, most days. This aspect of hospital life, would always lift your spirits.

No room at the Inn – thrown out to 5x.

Paralysis and weakness causes chair pushing to be extremely frustrating for relatively new cervical's without tricep control. This particular day, things had not run smoothly, I had just had a trying time getting back to the ward in time for the doctors weekly ward round, when it was announced that I was to be moved out to another ward. Furthermore, that this would make room for a new patient, who was arriving that afternoon. All my friends were in ward 2x and all my heartfelt pleas to stay with them, were rejected with an order to move me out forthwith.

Well, as you can imagine, a rather dejected
me, started pushing my chair out of the ward and
effectively, I felt homeless ! I realised that I was late
for my physio class and started wheeling in that
direction. As I reached the ward entrance my
wheelchair came to an abrupt halt, which was
caused by a vacuum cleaner lead, which was
stretched across the corridor floor. I hadn't got
enough strength left in my arms to get the wheels
to surmount it. At that instant another patient
pulled up behind me and shouted something like
'Hurry up, I've got to get out of the ward, I'm late
for my physio.' In reply, I blew up and blurted out '
Yeah, well you'll just have to fucking wait, won't
you, ' cause I can't get myself over this bastard of a
cable.'

A member of staff obligingly pushed my
chair over the cable and out into the corridor,
where I remained for half an hour or so... just
balling my eyes out.

I then realised that I had suffered one of
those rare moments and apologised to all who had
been within earshot of my foul language. I found
myself feeling somewhat depressed with the order
to move out of ward 2x. However, after crying my
eyes out, I was now feeling a little brighter and

realised that the news to move from one ward to another, had just brought things to a head. I was later informed that many patients suffering paralysis experienced depressive states of mind, during early stages of treatment. I was told by the ward sister that if I suffered feelings of depression again, that I should inform her or a doctor to have something done about it. I decided that the ward sister had given me sound advice.

My physio offered to introduce me to some of the cervicals in ward 5x and I in turn, regrettably, moved in that afternoon. My first impressions were that this was a dingy looking ward, but it was soon redecorated and it then became a ' home from home. ' I soon found that the ward orderlies were very capable and a very friendly bunch. One in particular was of Afro Caribbean descent, 6 foot 4 inches tall and made me feel very welcome from the start. He turned out to be a very keen horse racing fanatic, whose enthusiasm rubbed off on me, at which point I began pitching my doubtful wits against the bookies.

An orderly from another ward was the local bookies runner and his accent and manner made me regard him as being a member of the Mafia, although, I never discovered whether he was actually a Sicilian, a Greek Cypriot, a Spaniard or an Italian. He regularly took all the bets and the majority of patients spent more time crowded around the television watching the racing, than attending rehabilitation classes.

I was given the second bed on the right and the elderly chap in the first bed was in rather a pathetic state as he had been paralysed for almost thirty years and had developed ulcerated pressure sores. Some time later, I awoke one morning and noted that the elderly chaps bed was empty. He had passed away during the night and nothing more was said of him, as the ward staff had apparently been expecting him to pass away and he had now obliged them. Though, at the time, I found this acceptance of a mans death disconcerting to say the least.

Just along from me were three older patients in for pressure sore treatment. They knew each other well and they appeared to have developed the attitude that life was one long holiday and Stoke Mandeville was a holiday camp. During the summer months the beds were wheeled onto the lawns and this really contributed to the concept that the place was a holiday centre for wheelchair veterans.

The first was an Irishman, a back case, who was incessantly playing tape recordings of Jim Reeves ' albums. A headphone system was installed and loud music was banned, to assist in keeping the peace, on the wards. In response to this, the Irish gentleman overcame this by persistently singing along with Jim Reeves – loudly. His constant singing drove me completely mad.

In the bed next to him was a Greek Cypriot, who had been shot in the back, whilst involved in the British Army troubles out in Cyprus. His favourite ' taunt ' was that he had been shot in the back by the dirty British soldiers... but, we countered this by claiming that he must have caught a bullet, whilst running away. We later became great friends as he used to hold my playing cards for me whenever I was in bed and couldn't quite manage to ' handle ' them. He went on to marry the ward sister, but I was later informed that he died of a heart attack, just a few years later. On hearing the news I very much regretted mocking this lovely man, when we first met on the ward. I began to realise that death might not be far away, for patients who had suffered spinal injury.

The last of the trio was a young English lad who had broken his neck in a surfing accident, whilst he was off duty as a policeman in South Africa. He was nearing the beach when the mighty wave broke and he was simply ' wiped out ', as they say, breaking his neck as the tons of water smashed down onto him. He was a c5/6 and he regarded himself as a retired gentleman of independent means. He had been awarded a full pay pension for life and this allowed him to ' cock-a-snoot' at all and sundry. He was courting a nurse, at the time, but nothing came of it and I recently learned that he is living in a home somewhere in Hertfordshire.

Directly opposite to me there was a really grand old gentleman, who had broken his neck in a car crash. He just couldn't get over the fact that he had survived two World wars intact and then ' copped it ' as a result of a modern day invention, namely the motor vehicle. He was Victorian in character – addressing everyone as ' Old boy '. He told many a story of his travels around the world.

He once related how he had been a guest at an Arab wedding in the middle of the desert. Between gasps of his nearly obscene laughter, he told me of the tribesman's test of brides virginity on the wedding night... that involved the inserting of a pure white silk handkerchief, into the brides virgina – when a ' hoped for ' blood stained cloth was paraded all around the camp, resulting in great rejoicing. He never went on to say what would happen to a bride who had already been deflowered, which leaves me wondering what ' if any ' truth existed in his story and should we take it, with a pinch of salt.

This gentleman didn't hold back and informed everyone how he had lost a testicle, after it became infected and swollen. He was one of the incomplete cases, who could feel pain in various parts of his body. He pointed out that he had no regrets, at the passing of his testicle, adding that it had had its fair share of wear and tear. I'll leave the rest of that story for the reader to work out !

His general opinion was that life had soured during the fifties and sixties ! He explained that he was now Eighty Eight years of age, that his life was now drawing to a close and that he simply couldn't give a damn!

Next to him was a young man of Twenty Two years of age, who more than commiserated with me, as he had sustained a broken neck whilst practising somersaults on a trampoline at teacher training college. He was wearing a safety harness at the time, but miscalculated the speed of his somersault. The assistant who had been operating the harness, reacted too slowly, culminating in the young man landing hard and fast, breaking his neck on the metal framework of the trampoline. His level of neck break was c4/5, about an inch and a half higher than my own, which necessitated his being allocated an electric wheelchair, to get about in. He had sufficient arm movement to operate the electric control lever, but not enough to push a wheelchair.

Being what we refer to, medically, as an ' incomplete ' motor power lesion, enabled him to stand up without any leg supports, with someone aiding him to balance. He was incomplete all down one side and this caused his body to be pulled down on that side, giving him a hunch back appearance. This was caused by contractures, that are brought about by an operable muscle, pulling against an inoperable muscle. In my case for instance, my left arm bicep is a strong healthy muscle which is under my voluntary control, that causes my left arm to become slightly deformed at the elbow, because the bicep is not being counteracted by my tricep muscle at the back of the arm. Despite the fact that my tricep muscle was now wasting away, I had the opportunity to wear a splint which would help to counteract this effect.

On the other side of the coin my young friend couldn't use splints to counter his problem, because he had many of his body and trunk muscles working well. Unfortunately for him, these healthy muscles were pulling him over to one side. I concluded that paralysis is complicated and even more complicated when certain muscles are in fact still working !! I hope all you healthy people out there are grasping my explanations.

We discussed our accidents from time to time, when it was generally agreed that although trampoline and gymnastics in general, can be extremely dangerous, there was no need to ban these activities in schools and clubs, as long as expert supervision is maintained at all times!!

A glimpse at reality.

All new patients were expected to spend a weekend at home as soon as was possible after their accidents, in order that they should not become institutionalised. I'm beginning to sound like someone living under her Majesty's pleasure. I apologise to those who find my jokes somewhat limited.

It is a fearful ' step ' for a patient to have to
take and when it was suggested, at my five month
mark, that I should spend a weekend at home, I
promptly refused to go. After all... what did my
family know of evacuations, condoms and the like.

Well after much mind boggling adjustment I
actually warmed to the idea and it was eventually
arranged for me to have a full weekend's leave from
Friday to Sunday evening. My uncle Harry
Hawkins, who also lived in Aspland Grove, offered
to visit the hospital and take me home in his car.
My brother Michael accompanied Harry, both
arriving at about 4pm on the Friday evening. Not
having been home before I had to take all the
necessary equipment, which when seen by my
uncle, came as a bit of a shock.

To prevent me developing any pressure sores
I had been given the green light to take seven
pillows from my hospital bed, which would keep
me protected whilst sleeping on my own ordinary
domestic style bed. I also had to take my own
hospital mattress, because the welfare department
had not yet supplied me with a waterproof rubber
mattress. It had been agreed by my mother that an
evacuation would be carried out at home and to
this end I had to take twelve disposable

incontinence sheets, a packet of 25 plastic gloves, a large packet of cotton wool, a packet of cellulose wadding, a dozen suppositories and 200 grammes of senakot granules-some might say ' enough to move a mountain '.

For the waterworks: I had a Winchester bottle 'nothing to do with rifles by the way ' with a yard of of connecting tubing for night drainage, though plastic bags are now more commonly used. A spare ' kipper ', no, I'm not referring to a smoked herring, I don't want the older readers to get over excited. A kipper had the technical name ' supra-pubic bag ' which could be acquired from General practitioners, on form E C 10, from Genital Urinary Co. 28a, Devonshire Street, London, W.I.

If this starts to get boring-please let me know. For the uninitiated, I should explain that the kipper is a Black rubber bottle, which is used for the storage of a paralysed persons expressed urine. It would be strapped to your leg and worn under your trousers. When full the kipper could be emptied by means of a drainage tap situated at the bottom of the bottle. I also needed 6 spare condom sheaths, plus a tube of latex skin adhesive for holding them on. These incidentally were produced in Blackpool, Lancashire.

All of the items were then loaded up into my uncles car and I was then wheeled out, to be dutifully loaded up with the rest of the baggage. Crossing the car park the wind caught my sweating face and neck, prompting a series of shivers throughout my entire body. It struck me that life was not simply a bowl of cherries.

I didn't have a clue how best to get into the car and my 'worthy assistant ' didn't have a clue either, amazingly, my brother Michael suddenly picked me up out of the wheelchair and carried me to the front passenger seat, where Uncle Harry pulled my rear end into position. I was now sitting in a car seat feeling rather dishevelled, but maybe with a hint of anticipation.

One of the old 'sweats ' on my ward had told me to ignore mishaps and just get off home. Well, now that I was in the car, I knew exactly what he had been hinting at. My trousers were virtually off, my shirt and pullover were up around my chest, and my bulging tummy was on full display. Nevertheless, my chaperone's put me back together the best they could and after they finally discovered how to collapse the wheelchair, we set off, homeward bound.

A Split Second Accident

Seat belts were not compulsorily fitted then and I went through shear hell trying all sorts of ways to support myself during braking and cornering. The windows were wide open and that caused me to sweat incessantly. The resultant tenseness was unbelievable, although, at that time, I never new the cause.

The girls were out in full force, though, unfortunately we were all eyeing them to intently, as my uncle had to hit the brakes at a set of red traffic lights. Being over six foot tall, my trunk was shot forwards and my face smashed against the dashboard, fortunately, I was unhurt, although shaken by the experience. The car was of medium size, which left my legs bent up, which resulted in the waterworks having to flow uphill. Half way through the trip a severe leak was discovered and by the time we reached home I had cursed the orderlies a thousand times for not having connected the condom on properly. My lovely Uncle Harry's car was now swimming in urine and you can only imagine how this left me feeling.

My lovely Mum came up to the car to greet me, but I could only request that she remove the mattress quickly from the car, as I urgently needed a new condom fitting. I was then lifted into my wheelchair and realised that all the neighbours and children in the street, had gathered to witness the spectacle. I was wheeled into my house looking like a dishevelled mess, with my tummy bared to the world, stinking of urine and literally soaked from head to toe. It was not my finest hour, I had arrived home and what a right bloody state I had arrived in.

Once in the house my two eldest brothers attempted fitting their first condom on me and although it was a poor job, due to me incessantly urinating, we all agreed that it would have to do, for the first night. I then enjoyed a meal of sausages and chips prepared by my Mum of course, after which our well meaning neighbours arrived one after the other, on good will visits. This was very much appreciated, but left me completely exhausted when finally retiring to bed, after mid night. I felt that my first day of freedom had passed off quite well, but was very relieved as the bedroom light was switched off.

No sooner had I closed my eyes, my mother woke me to carry out my first bed turn. The last thing mum wanted was for me to return to the hospital on Sunday, with a bedsore. Mum spent the

next half hour in turning me over to perfection.
She checked that the head pillows were positioned
correctly, that the hip pillows were ironed out
sufficiently, that my legs were positioned correctly
and that the waterworks tubing was straightened
out enough for easy flow during the remaining
hours of the night.

At 7 am. mum woke me, with bleary eyes,
and started the next bed turn. She was then
abruptly fully awakened by the fact that the
condom had become completely detached, from,
you know where. The bedding of course was
soaked through. Mum set about fitting and gluing
the new condom in place and then had to fully
dress me. She then summoned my two older
brothers from their cosy retreats, who then lifted
me from the bed into the wheelchair. They both
showed off for being awoken early and my name
was mud for the rest of the day.

In the afternoon my parents wanted to take
me out around the local shops, but my fear of the
wind and the cold made me opt for the television
and the fire. Later that day an old girlfriend came
to visit me and offered to push me in the
wheelchair to her parents house. I declined her
offer on the basis that it was a little early for me to

go visiting people. I suppose I lacked confidence
and needed more time with my family.
Unfortunately she didn't understand my reluctance
to go and after saying her goodbyes she left, never
to return again.

In the evening my brothers had mellowed
and offered to take me out for a pint, when, to their
surprise, I refused to go. They couldn't understand
my fear of springing a leak in public and they didn't
know that I was basically very reluctant to bump
into any old friends, as I was regarding myself as
being somewhat of a freak to look at with my
bulging tummy and sweaty face. There is a genuine
fear experienced by new cases that have to face this
step back into public life and I later discovered that
numerous other cases had felt the same as I had.

It was a year or so before I began to venture
out, although, now knowing the situation for what
it is, I would strongly advise any new cases to let
leaks and the like go to hell, as it does no good
putting off getting back into public life. It must
come one day and the sooner the better!

At around ten, I had to swallow a revolting
dose of senokot granules... and during the night
turn we discovered I'd had an early action. In the
morning a very tired looking mother decided I had

had an insufficient result and it was therefore lunchtime before we had gotten evacuations out of the way and me up and dressed.

The situation was that although we had an inside toilet it was not accessible and we thus had to deal with evacuation in bed. Back cases and lower lesion cases can make use of a toilet, or even a commode if this is necessary. But in my circumstances at that time a commode would have served no useful purpose as the living room was next to our dining room and the smell of excreta would have still been present. It was not a funny situation and it was not conducive to anyone's appetite for Sunday lunch, to say the least.

By tea time I was feeling that I had been such a heavy burden to my family (in more ways than one), that I was happy to be returning to Stoke Mandeville. I felt that they at least, were receiving payment for looking after me!

After saying my goodbyes to my lovely mum, Michael again lifted me into Harry's car and before I knew it, we were well on our way back to Stoke. As we neared the hospital, good old Uncle Harry insisted on buying me a pint, which I enjoyed in the car. I was again feeling dishevelled after being man handled into the car seat, but the lager

cheered me up... no end!! By Nine o'clock I was
back in the ward, where, once again, I discovered
that the condom had come amiss and of course I
was soaking wet. I now cursed myself for having
had that wonderful pint of lager. I was soon sorted
by the staff and on speaking to two other lads on
the ward, found that they had also escaped for the
weekend. I found that they had also suffered the
same miserable problems with urination and
condom failings.

We of course, all felt very sorry for ourselves,
in thinking that we were doomed to an existence of,
as one of the more poetical of the lads put it,
always pissing and shitting ourselves. please, do
forgive us, if offended in any way by our ' poetic
licence '. I wish to point out that without this
banter, we would all go completely bonkers.

I knew, at that time, that the basic reason for
our persistently getting wet was caused by the
condoms not being glued on properly in the first
place. And so, I kept as sharp an eye as I could on
whoever happened to be fitting one on. But I still
became wet every time I was being lifted in or out
of a car? So, after much consultation with old cases
I discovered that this was being caused by the legs
swinging into an extremely bent position when a

lift took place. The heavy ' Kipper ' pulled on the short connecting tubing and pulled the condoms off. I hope you've all been paying attention and recall that the ' kipper ' is not a smoked fish, but a urine bag.

A slightly longer length of tubing, coupled with emptying the bag prior to a lift, virtually cut out this source of misery. Most of us of course couldn't feel the wetness, but we could certainly smell it. It was at about this time, that I settled down at Stoke, becoming daily, more used to the idea that I was now a disabled person. As you can only imagine, this was a tough realisation to come to terms with. I had lost about three stone in weight, in the first 6 months of paralysis. The shocking fact is that most of the weight loss related to lost muscle, now seeing your bones, where muscle once sat, was quite upsetting. However, in the main, the wonderful physio's would keep our spirits up and bring us through.

Reflecting back on my first home visit, I feel that I was quite lucky with my home being readily accessible to a wheelchair. There are many cases who have to be carried up a flight of steps to gain access to a terraced house, or up several flights of stairs to get into a flat where there are no lifts available. I know of cases that have had to have huge ramps fitted, one chap who had to have a lift fitted and another who had an electrically operated moving platform fitted to his staircase. Extensive household alterations are frequently needed and occasionally whole house extensions to create extended or new rooms.

Usually, the hospitals almoners have looked into the accessibility of one's accommodation, prior to your being able to go home, but often alterations take many months or even a year, before completion of the work. This often results in the case in question, remaining in Stoke until the home is made ready for them. If the individual has money, there are rarely any hold ups, but, if a local council are carrying out the work, things can be very slow in becoming completed. I feel that these Councils really should put a great deal more money and manpower into these jobs, than they do at present!

Although my house was thought to be unsuitable in the long term, it was thought to be just manageable for me to come home at weekends and we were promised a new accommodation from the council, as soon as was possible. Finally, however, after many months and four unsuitable council house offers, it was decided to carry out alterations at the house I lived in, prior to my accident. A kitchen to the rear of our house would be turned into my bedroom and the local Rotary Club chipped in to assist the Council with their limited funds. In other words the Council would not release sufficient funds to complete the work.

Prior to the completion of the work, during subsequent visits home, my family members had to set my bed up and take it down each evening in our living room. Sheets and pillow cases were then left about , not to mention the urine bottle and fluff tended to settle everywhere. It all had to be cleared away and the room would then be hoovered. Mum pointed out that although she could manage at weekends with the help of the family, it would be impossible for her to manage on her own, during weekdays. As a result of this dilemma, I remained at Stoke for a total of two years and two months, whilst the local bureaucrats were very slowly working towards completion of my home alteration work.

In fairness, I suppose I should add that I had a long way to go, in any event, before I would be fit and ready for returning home on a full time basis.

Hydrotherapy.

After having been up and about in a wheelchair for a few weeks most patients were allowed to do a full days rehabilitation, throughout the various departments. This entailed physiotherapy, occupational therapy, hydrotherapy, archery and table tennis. Of course, a given case could only take part in these classes as far as his physical capabilities would permit, but it was truly astonishing to discover just how much could be achieved. I couldn't believe that cases at my level were able to do archery and table tennis, as I was convinced they must be much better off physically, but, many were in a similar state as myself. I'm now thinking, ' exciting times ahead '!! - but, hey lets not get carried away.

Hydrotherapy or swimming classes were attended twice a week, but in certain circumstances a case could be authorised to attend for as many sessions as was thought necessary. I had heard that there was a swimming gala held during the paraplegic games and having been a good swimmer prior to my accident, I was keen on showing everyone what a great competitor I would make for the games.

The classes were held in the morning, which meant that the patients wouldn't have to be dressed twice. We would be put into our wheelchairs straight from the bed and then wheeled off to the swimming pool. A pyjama jacket was left on and a blanket was placed in the chair to be wrapped around your waist and legs. Although, the blanket frequently made it difficult to get to the pool on time, as it persistently got caught up in the wheels and brakes.

At the edge of the pool were two lifts for transferring people into the water. One was short for people who could balance sufficiently to be sat up and the other was long, for people who couldn't sit up and had to be layed out. The auxiliary staff lifted the patients onto the lift, which was then raised up above the pool wall and down into the water, where a physio would be waiting to float her patient off into the water. I'm pleased to inform you that some of the Physio's wore very sexy costumes and it was very enjoyable for the male contingent to be carried in the arms of an attractive young women.

I'm sure that the physios were aware of our admiration and also understood that ' boys will be boys ' whenever possible, some might say ' all part of the recovery programme '.

Getting back to more mundane matters, the incontinent waterworks were dealt with by the women expressing their bladder on the loo prior to leaving the ward and the men leaving their condoms on. The short connecting tube would be shut off by means of a spigot in the end or a clamp screwed onto it and it was then tucked away inside the swimming trunks. Thus, if a patient did happen to pass water whilst in the pool the condom would simply inflate and it could be drained off, once the patient had been reunited with the wheelchair. There were a few red faces occasionally, whenever we were lifted out on the lift, with a huge bulge under the trunks. The good news was that the staff normally knew what the problem was which resulted in it being treated with a good laugh all round.

On entering the pool, I found myself very disappointed with my swimming ability, as for some odd reason I had assumed that although I was paralysed, I would still be able to swim. I had built up grand mental pictures of myself cruising up and down the pool and when this hadn't materialised, I felt rather like a child who had been refused some sweets. I could move my arms and trunk, at which point my legs floated, but I could only swim a few yards. This wasn't what I would have called swimming, in my pre accident days. Well, the expected miracle from the cure – all hydrotherapy classes hadn't come about and I was very annoyed with myself for having let my imagination run away with me.

I tried swimming on my back, by throwing both arms above my head whilst my physio supported me from the side. This seemed to work at which point I asked her to let me attempt it on my own. Alas, the floating legs and trunk persistently forced my face back below the water mark and I was unable to breath sufficiently. I then attempted a form of front crawl, but I couldn't use my arms well enough from the elbows, to allow me to throw them forwards far enough to get a reasonable stroke. I was again unable to lift my head out of the water to allow for breathing.

I moaned that it was going to be impossible for me to swim without being able to breathe, when my physio was quick to point out that many cases of my level encountered difficulties when they first attempted swimming, but they eventually found a means of swimming which suited their individual arm muscle control variations.

As it was, the secret of being able to 'swim' lay in forgetting about breathing, at least for a moment or two. I was layed face down in the water with my arms out in front, forming a semi circle. When I drew them in towards my chest, I was propelled slightly forward. It wasn't a very efficient means of swimming, but it was a means of making a little headway.

We agreed that after a few strokes I should lie still and she would turn me over so I could breathe again. Alas, women being the gregarious creatures they are, I almost drowned on several occasions. I would take a breath and then be put onto my front to take a few strokes, but she would turn round for a natter with a colleague. Having completed my effort and run out of air, I would lie still for a few seconds. When nothing happened I would splash my arms about in the water in an effort to gain a breath, when she would look around and see me still 'swimming' and continue with her chat. By this time, being desperate, I would be wildly splashing about trying to get some air. Looking round again she would remark something about how keen I was today!! Finally, when I was almost a goner, she would realise just how long I'd been face down and would then come and turn me over. All I could do was to have, an, hysterical laugh about it.

The fact is that all the twisting and squirming in the world is insufficient to cause a c5/6 quads lower trunk and legs to roll over in the water. The paralysis from the upper chest down prevents the shoulder and arm efforts from having any rolling effect on your body, whenever you attempt to roll over in such a situation. However, I finally solved the breathing problem when I discovered that I could slip my forearms into the water gulley running around the inside of the pool brickwork. I could gain sufficient arm leverage to lift my mouth clear of the water to enable me to breathe. I often slipped off this gulley and took in many mouthfuls of water instead.

Apart from being used for swimming lessons the pool was used as a general hydrotherapy unit. The warm water helped stiff joints to loosen up, therefore, incomplete patients could readily exercise muscles or limbs that were still under their voluntary control. A person with weak leg muscles could be stood in the pool with the buoyancy of the water until eventually the muscles might develop to the state whereby they could stand up outside the pool. Numerous incomplete cases experienced a great deal of pain after having spent three months or more cramped up in bed, therefore, the warmth of the water allowed them to ease their muscles back into use with as little pain as possible.

Many elderly incomplete cases had perhaps been suffering from crippling diseases, such as rheumatism or arthritis, prior to their accidents which could be contributing to their limited ability of movement as well as their partial paralysis. The warm water enabled them to exercise their joints with relative ease. A man's legs are often very heavy and when a complete motor power case cannot exercise them himself it makes it much easier for the physio to carry out any passive movements in the pool.

Even complete motor power cervical cases can feel pain in their shoulders, therefore, any discomfort can be minimised when their shoulders are eased back into limited use in the comfort of the pool. So, as you can see, the pool treatment can be beneficial to a vast number of varying cases, all of whom can benefit from hydrotherapy to some degree.

When a session in the pool was over the physio floated her patient back onto the appropriate lift for him or her to be hoisted back into their chair. Obviously, the lifts are sited in the open and this can often cause some embarrassment as trunks were removed before you were taken off of the lift. A quick dry off is then administered by a student nurse or auxiliary and you are then reconnected to your urine drainage bag and wrapped in a blanket ready for the push back to the ward. I should point out, that the ladies are seen to behind a screen.

In fact, it was not the sexual aspect which caused me concern at that stage but the point that all the males looked as if they were permanently eight months pregnant with their bulging tummies. This made a lot of men self conscious and it discouraged them from attending the pool as often as they should, though it did take a great deal of ribbing to prevent them from attending the pool for a cuddle with their physiotherapist.

The push back to the ward was particularly difficult for cases at my level because we were as incapacitated as one could be without it being necessary to be issued with an electric chair. Cases below c5/6 such as c5 or c 4/5, could get around much easier in their electric chairs. What with the blanket getting continually caught up and my being weak after a swim anyway, I often wished I had been left more or less severely incapacitated in order to have been issued with an electric chair or been able to move myself around better than I was currently able to do.

On finally making it back to the ward at around lunchtime, you would be severely reprimanded in Spanish or Italian for being late back followed by some rough handling to get you dressed and back in your chair before lunch was served up. The difficulty was, the condoms needed changing after becoming blown up or unstuck in the pool. What with the ward sister urging them to hurry up, the orderlies didn't think it was worth bothering with such a task. However, a ward sisters bark is worse than her bite and a sharp cervical will stick to his guns and insist the condom be changed or he will discover he nearly always gets wet trousers the afternoon after a swimming session. So, when you are hurriedly thrown into your wheelchair in a mess, you can console yourself, that at least you are likely to remain dry for the remainder of the day.

Occupational Therapy.

Many an enjoyable hour could be spent in the O.T. department. Although perhaps the term ' O.T. department ' is slightly an incorrect description of this part of the hospital, as it was a general rehabilitation department. The department consisted of five minor departments within itself-the engineering shop, the woodwork shop, the typing pool, the kitchen and general O.T. Area. A patients involvement in any particular department depended very much on the individual's physical limitations.

Personally, I received more rehabilitation than I could handle, and during my second year in particular, all I wanted to do was sit around in the canteen or corridors and watch the girls go by. However, as mine was a typical case of rehabilitating a complete motor power c5/6, I shall relate to what went on in my early months in this department.

In my first few weeks I was introduced to the dubious delights of tray making. Trays and mosaic lamp stands were turned out by the dozen, although, the intricate work on the lamp stands was a little beyond the physical capacities of cervicals, so we concentrated more on the trays. At my level an arm had to be used for balance, leaving only one paralysed hand free, for work, which usually needed a minimum of eight fingers and two thumbs in good working order.

The strands to be woven for the sides of the tray would constantly spring back up and I often got a face full of points, whenever I forgot about balance and fell flat on my face; but, a small price to pay, for the glory of one day completing one's very own tray. This type of work was definitely beneficial to developing the knack of using one's seemingly useless hands, even though they hadn't actually any gripping power.

Being summer time made it rather warm and me being a sweat case already made it difficult to concentrate on the work ' in hand ' with the sweat constantly dripping off my nose and chin. Nonetheless, I managed to complete two trays (which I still have). Alas, I then decided that tray making was no longer of interest to me, as I was convinced I could draw no further benefit from that particular source of 'amusement'.

The engineering shop never interested me much as there was very little I could 'handle' with regard to the heavy tools and metals. The lathes and benches had been built low enough to be operated on from a wheelchair and the back cases, or even some of the low lesion cervicals, were often seen to be doing light engineering work. Whether it was for recreation or rehabilitation the engineering shop was always being put to good use.

The carpentry shop was next door and here again were lathes for turning work, as well as the expected wood turning tools and benches. This workshop was more popular with the quadriplegics, because the tools and materials were a little lighter to 'handle' with, limited grip in one's hands. The work was looked upon, as being, more of a recreation than a means of earning a living, after discharge, although I do know of a back case, who left to earn a decent living knocking out dozens of coffee tables.

When a quadriplegic had been set up on a lathe, he could be left to get on with turning a fruit bowl or lamp stand with a reasonable degree of safety, to both himself and others in the shop. Perhaps ironically, whenever a bunch of visitors were informed that a given lad turning a bowl hadn't actually any grip in the hands, you could always detect a somewhat incredulous look in many an eye. Yet, the fact is, a quadriplegic usually looks just as whole bodied as a paraplegic, even though the latter has normal grip and the former does not.

Before attempting to do any work in the shop I knew that the effort would serve to increase my sweating, but as I eventually became very bored with hospital life, I decided to give a fruit bowl a try, regardless. I had to maintain balance very carefully, to avoid falling onto the spinning job and I eventually discovered that my support arm could be advantageously positioned to give the chisel some support. I couldn't exert much pressure, but a little tool feed caused the machine to do the cutting.

The wooden chippings began to fly and the sweat began to pour. My face was not 15 inches from the ' bowl to be ' and each and every wood chipping was hitting me straight in the face and sticking to it. They worked their way down my neck and inside my shirt, when, before long, I was just one sticky prickly mess, with any slight movement causing dozens of wood shavings to stick into me. There was no getting away from them or the sweat and after half an hour's work I had to push back to the ward to be changed.

However, I was reluctant to quit and stuck with it, 'please pardon the pun', until the bowl had been turned. All I had to do now was sand and polish it. Easier said than done, the wood dust shot everywhere... mostly into my face and I frequently emerged from the shop looking as though hundreds of hours of dust had been allowed to settle over me. On the last occasion I had to sand the bowl I had a slight accident. My left hand was red and sore, caused by the heat generated from friction; but, as I couldn't feel any pain I didn't concern myself. I momentarily looked away from the job and when I looked back again, I discovered two of my knuckles to be bared to the bone. The sandpaper had slipped out and my hand had been rubbing against my spinning bowl.

It was a curious experience to see that my hand had unknowingly been cut to pieces, which should serve as a lesson for all paraplegics and quadriplegics wherever they haven't any feeling. One can sustain a burn or a scald all to easily and therefore , you should stay well away from the likes of electric or coal fires and for that matter, radiators. Frostbite can also cause damage wherever there is no feeling, so this should be watched for whenever one is exposed to intense cold.

Eventually, I got around to polishing the bowl, which I still have and cherish. Perhaps... because my very flesh and blood went into its making, it may be highly valued.

Up to level c5/6, handwriting can be managed, although some cervicals will have to make use of gadgets early on. I t depends on the individual, but eventually all such aids can be dispensed with and one should have found some means of fixing a pen in the paralysed fingers to be able to write. Fountain and ballpoint pens cause difficulty in one's keeping an even flow of ink on the paper, so felt tipped pens are much preferred. Speed and legibility are different to attain, as one's whole arm has to be moved across the paper, when you frequently end up with disjointed words. However, I, personally, write very little because I have found I can get away with someone else doing the leg work and I then just add my signature.

A few months after I had been up I was given an electric typewriter by an external charity organisation (Thank you whoever you are) at which time I started learning to type. Of course fingers and thumbs couldn't be used, so a stick (a plonker) was strapped onto my palm to assist me in typing. I was then encouraged to attain a reasonable speed of typing, by ' plonking ' away at one letter key at a time.

Laborious... not in the least! Originally, I was knocking out six to eight words to the minute, although I can now manage thirty to thirty five, depending on how well I want the work to look. Some lower level cervicals can type with a plonker in each palm and still maintain balance and thus can type much faster. But this is only advantageous if one happens to be doing any form of copying work.

Setting margins always presented me with problems as there were two keys on opposite sides of the typewriter which have to be simultaneously depressed. If two plonkers are being used, margins could be set, but with only one, difficulties continued to frustrate the individual. I eventually adopted the means of depressing the margin setter key with my plonker and the spacer bar with my tongue. How inelegant-some might say?

Getting the paper in is also difficult as the thin paper slips out between the fore finger and thumb, once the wrist has been cocked. Once in the carriage the paper frequently falls out again before you can depress the automatic feed-in key or wind it in manually (not an easy task) and therefore, as a bit of ' cunning ' always wins the day, a little spittle on the paper will be found sufficient to hold the paper momentarily in place until it can be fed in.

Patients of level c5 or c4/5 are able to type with the aid of a long 'plonker' held in the mouth. And for those above this level, who can move very little, there is a machine set-up, known as P.O.S.S.U.M. which enables them to be able to type. A pipe like mouthpiece is connected to an intricate system of minute diaphragms, operating the keys by various combinations of blows and sucks.

P.O.S.S.U.M. was later adapted for home use, operating such things around the house such as lighting, heating, alarm bells, television, radio, phone, intercom etc. and generally, anything which the patient couldn't operate himself could be fitted into the system, although, such intricate tasks as changing long playing records on a Hi- Fi, were a little beyond its scope.

It can be provided free on The National Health, via your G. P for all who are in obvious need of it. In fact there are people who are using hand operated systems, who are not quite so severely incapacitated, as having such a system to hand can exclude a great deal of the drudgery involved with having to push around the house every few minutes to answer the front door, for example. One push and the door opens.

A magazine is circulated amongst the users and there are great friendships engendered between those that are incapacitated enough to merit the issue of such a machine. Users find that all the difficulties and frustrations they are encountering have been experienced previously by others and therefore, all users should subscribe to the magazine.

P O S S U M machine users were usually introduced to the machine in the typing pool. During the mornings basic commerce lessons were given here and in the afternoons the very high cases were left in peace to blow and suck whilst perhaps typing a letter to their relatives. My typewriter was eventually moved into this room and from time to time I was allowed to go in and type whatever I wished. 'Plonking' away at the typewriter could be very therapeutic in itself and whenever I was finding life particularly irksome I could go to the typing pool and have it out on my typewriter, plonking away until my heart was content.

After I had been doing this for a year or so the O.T staff decided that I should be given something more constructive to do with my time and they therefore arranged for me to have an aptitude test for computer programming, with a view to this being a possible source of employment, on discharge from the hospital.

Well, I passed the test with flying colours and was given a tape recorder by another external charity, to enable me to complete the programming course which had been read onto tape. A guy with a broad American accent started balling at me through my headphones and any difficulties I encountered were to be replayed to be crystal clear. I kept up with him for the first few tapes...what with having to switch the typewriter on and off and feed numerous sheets of paper in and out of the typewriter etc.

I even managed to understand him to about two thirds of the way through, although, I must admit that by this time I was just listening instead of fighting to get all the format forms in and out of the typewriter. But, alas, by the end he had lost me and I had to admit that I wasn't destined to become the greatest computer programming wizard of all time.

Finally, after listening to all of the tapes a few times I didn't wish to admit to being too thick to be able to understand the course, so I told the staff that programming appeared to be beyond my physical abilities and I was glad that they allowed me to give it up, as a bad job.

Nonetheless, the fact that I had been given a four track tape-recorder was sufficient compensation for me to swallow my pride. I eventually put it to good use by having hours of music recorded on tape. There wasn't anywhere else available for playing loud music at that time and therefore, whenever the unit wasn't in use a few patients gathered around the tape to have a rather pathetic sing along. But it was a good means of our letting off some steam.

From time to time our chats developed into serious discussion, when, perhaps inevitably, the subject discussed was that of ' Euthanasia '. This particular topic arose because it was of great relevance to the P O S S U M machine users, consisting of the most severely paralysed individuals in the whole spinal unit. The general consensus eventually boiled down to being that all cervical cases (those paralysed in all four limbs) should be given the choice as to whether the individual would like to quietly ' bow out ' with dignity, that is, however,   (which was not apparent to either myself or those others involved in the discussion) that it is the first few years which are both physically and emotionally the most difficult to endure.

A given case may well wish to' throw in the towel ' early on, before he has realised that life can be made enjoyably fascinating and rewarding, no matter under what particularly difficult set of circumstances it has to be lived.

The choice should not be given to such cases, for the reason mentioned above and, because it would inevitably be a highly emotionally influenced decision at such an early stage, in their recovery. But, of course, for numerous other forms of illnesses, disabilities, and diseases the question is very much open to debate.

The kitchen unit was set out in such a way as to prove to the previously ordinary everyday housewives that they could still achieve a great deal if things were layed out to accommodate them physically. Adaptation, is the key word and if work tops, sink units, ovens, and cupboards and the ' like ', are all adapted for use by a chair-bound housewife, even cervical women are often amazed at what they can still achieve, with regard to the culinary arts.

Admittedly, a multi course dinner would be a little beyond their resources, but I'll never forget the faces of two particular young women, both complete motor power cervicals, when they were seen to emerge from the kitchen with a cake apiece on their laps.

Physiotherapy. The Circus.

As with my swimming, I was extremely disappointed with my early efforts in the physio departments. I had unwittingly assumed it was just a case of my having to get my previously strong muscles back into shape. When I found out there was precious little I could do the fact hit me like a sledgehammer blow.

I had great difficulty in hauling even two pounds up and down on the arm pulleys. I couldn't quite manage to lift a leg up onto a plinth top and it would take me fifteen minutes to pull a sweater on

or off whilst putting up with the frustration of
continually overbalancing all over the place.

It was claimed at the time that cervicals of my
level and below should eventually be capable of
dressing their top halves on their own. Although I
agree that this is possible it was another thing I
could not do as without tricep control this task was
much to time consuming and exhausting.

During my early weeks in the physio
departments it was first brought home to me that it
was not only men who were open to sustaining
spinal injuries. There were women and children in
the same condition as myself. There were children
of two or three years of age and females from
perhaps ten to eighty years of age. Absolutely
nobody appeared to be exempt from sustaining a
broken neck or back. It seemed to me that only the
men should have had to undergo such a traumatic
experience. The fact that these emotionally weaker
females had to go through it, was to my mind, an
unfair deal that had been indiscriminately handed
out to them by the gods.

The irony of the situation was that all the
children treated it as a big game, in which they
were forever playing about, as kids do. Most of the

women that were seen to be struggling regularly
with whatever tasks they were set to do appeared to
have accepted their plight as being their just
desserts for having committed some long past
unspoken of crimes. Many times I would curse
myself for not being able to accomplish some
simple task. Each and every time I did so my heart
went out to the women and girls and the wild
young kids.

An odd situation was, however, that virtually
all the young children had sustained back breaks
and they were therefore all extremely mobile. They
could use their hands and could propel themselves
around the corridors and departments at an almost
terrifying speed. Although I was happy to see them
whizzing about everywhere I often found myself
being resentfully jealous, a feeling which was later
related to me as having been experienced by other
cervical cases.

As the days passed and I came to know more
and more people, it seemed that the atmosphere of
true friendship was always on the increase.
Everyone, it seemed, had realised that we were
completely in the soup and as we were all in it
together, what the hell did it matter. We all had to
laugh at our tragically pathetic situations and we

therefore all accepted it and got on with it as best we could.

The physical difficulties to be overcome were considerable and it had to be accepted that these were not going to be surmounted by any great strides in our physical improvement but by our adopting knacks in accomplishing things in ways we could not as yet fully comprehend.

Some of the people who had not done a good job of breaking their neck or back, the incomplete motor cases, were capable of achieving a great deal more than were their counterparts. At level c5 and above, very little could be done physically and in a way this didn't matter much as these people could get about well in their electric chairs. They had to have virtually everything else done for them. The back cases were capable of doing most things for themselves except for having a walkabout. The low lesion neck cases were capable, in time to do most things except for dressing their bottom half, unless of course, one was exceptionally adept.

It was when we came to my level of injury, c5/6 that a great many tasks had to be painstakingly accomplished. There is no balance, no tricep muscle control and only weak biceps and wrist ex tensors. We were expected to be able to dress our top half, wash and feed ourselves, push around well and transfer onto a plinth top balance, ease our backside pressure build up and get on and off a bed. Also, when the time was right, to get into or out of a car.

First, you had to learn some method of easing the backside pressure build up, in order to prevent it from breaking out in sores. This was a much more difficult task than it might at first sound. This is because the arms cannot be readily brought into a straightened position against the weight of ones body or for that matter against the slightest pull of gravity.

I have frequently been asked why I haven't any control over my tricep arm muscles when it can clearly be seen that I can move my arms in any direction I wish. Well the fact is that the loss of control over this set of arm muscles does not become apparent until one needs to acquire something from above head height. It then becomes obvious that the area cannot be supported from the elbow. The nerves come off of the spinal cord to operate the triceps from just below the level of my lesion, therefore, any brain impulses to these muscles to move, get to the break and can travel no further, so the muscles never receive any message to move.

Right, to get back to lifting, the main problem arises from the fact that every time you attempt to lift, you overbalance and therefore have to wrack your brain to discover a method of lifting to suit your own individual physical abilities. In my case I eventually found a means of lifting whilst maintaining my balance by propping my elbow on my chair armrest and pushing down with my hand against the tyre from behind my chair-back. With the arm being externally rotated in this way, pressure could be applied against the arm and I could lift the right buttock with the right arm and left elbow and the left buttock with the left arm and right elbow.

Being tall though, my trunk would elongate, leaving my backside on the cushion. It wasn't until I was able to lift about four inches or more that I was able to ease the pressure sufficiently. In the early days you need to lift every half hour but the skin on your backside toughens in time and you are able to sit for perhaps sixteen hours a day without any ill effects. This being said, it is still essential to move frequently to maintain good skin at all times. For cervicals of c5 and above, who are incapable of lifting themselves, there are electronically controlled inflatable air cushions.

Upper body balance has to be gained and the difficulties involved with this problem cannot be fully understood unless it is realised that a cervical case has no control over the trunk muscles that would normally support a person sitting in an upright position. Unless he or she can see whether they are squarely balanced, a cervical will be unable to feel that he or she is about to fall off balance and therefore will just keep going and fall completely over. Apart from the fact that you cannot sit up again without assistance, it is very disconcerting to be ungraciously sprawled out like a helpless rag doll.

For this reason a full length mirror is placed in front of the patient whilst he or she is sat with their legs over the edge of a plinth. This allows the patient to see whether he or she is sat squarely or falling off balance. Alas, I had been avoiding a good look into one of these large mirrors as I had been reluctant to actually take a look at what a bloody state I was in. I now had to get used to the idea as I was to be sat in front of one for virtually every day for the following five or six weeks. I was covered in huge pussy spots and my hair was sticking up all over the place and two plaster dressings where my calipers had been. But, as some sarcastic lad often shouted, we weren't there to win any beauty contests!

When off balance you had to counterbalance by an appropriate head or arm movement. The physio was sat close by to ensure you didn't end up in a heap on the floor. The whole thing developed into a bizarre game with the physio continually knocking you off balance whilst you had to counterbalance.

Side to side falling was easy to see and it was accordingly the easiest to counter. Backwards or forwards was more difficult to be aware of and it was more difficult to counter. The head is very heavy and therefore it is important to make good use of it in balance control. From time to time you would forget about this and when suddenly looking around to talk to someone would fall completely off balance.

In time I was able to balance quite well and I could then counter even my physio who gave me a reasonable push. To improve balance further the physio staff took to running a morning class in which we were all sat on the floor in a circle to practice the throwing and catching of balls. The ball nearly always knocked me off balance although I couldn't actually catch it anyhow. I persistently got knocked backwards, banging my head on the floor. Although I didn't mind the bumps to much I could never quite get used to that feeling of falling over backwards into oblivion.

I eventually realised that it was because our legs were positioned out straight that we were being forced over backwards to easily but when we had them opened widely I was able to catch the ball without falling backwards and bumping my head. With balancing problems having been partially overcome, we were to be stirred to greater heights of attainment in the near future.

The next problem to be overcome was that of transferring from a wheelchair onto a plinth top. You had to maintain balance during any exertions as a sudden nod of the head in the wrong direction could result in you being sprawled out in an odd fashion and most probably on the floor. Whenever this did occur and it often did, it was necessary for three or four of the staff to be rounded up to get six foot me back into my much loved wheelchair to be wheeled off for a check up by honourable doctor to see if any bones had been unknowingly broken under the weight of the fall. We were similar to

helpless young babies and in fact we needed our
nappies changing just as frequently as a baby does.
All the lifting from chair to floor and back again
often ended up with an unavoidable bowel
movement or springing a waterworks leak.

Well, the legs could be lifted onto the plinth
top and the trunk gotten across after or the trunk
could be gotten over first leaving the legs to be
dragged on later, if or when you had regained
sufficient energy and "puff" to do so. With regard
to this leg-lifting aspect, I considered myself to be
particularly unlucky as the majority of patients had
legs that had wasted away to a considerable extent
yet mine were as muscle-bound as they had been at
the time of my accident. This made it more
difficult for me to even lift a foot up off of a chair
let alone lift both legs up onto a plinth top for
transferring.

I tried every possible combination of lifting
my legs up onto the plinth top but in each and
every case I found that I was greatly in need of a
third arm. One arm was hooked around the chair
backrest handle for balancing whilst the other was
hooked under a knee for lifting. A third arm was
actually needed for getting the foot onto the plinth

top once the leg had been raised high enough. I tried sitting sideways on to the side of the plinth, sideways on to the end and head on to both the side and end, all to no avail.

After several weeks of trying to get my feet up onto the plinth top first, I finally decided to attempt to get my trunk over first and then try and haul the legs on. But alas, this method was no use either. Everything seemed to be against my being able to transfer. If it wasn't lack of tricep control, it was not being able to balance sufficiently during the transfer. If it wasn't for the shear weight of my legs it was my elongated trunk, which persistently left my backside sitting stubbornly on the chair cushion as if it wanted nothing to do with the job in hand.

However, the ability of being able to transfer successfully was eventually revealed to me by my physio in the shape of one "sliding board". This short, highly polished board bridged the gap between my chair and plinth and my backside could then be literally slid onto the plinth top.

Several months later and with a great deal of perseverance and heartfelt encouragement from my physio, I was eventually able to transfer and get my legs over as well without frequently overbalancing or falling onto the floor.

Concerning my ability to transfer onto a bed, I believe my physio took pity on me and gave up the idea of its ever being a practical possibility. A bed is much higher than a plinth top and the bed linen catches your backside, so preventing a successful transfer unless of course you are capable of lifting the backside absolutely clear.

Actually, if there are cervicals keen enough to persist with getting themselves into and out of bed after they have been discharged, the clue to making the task much easier lies in obtaining a bed with adjustable height control. This can be lowered below chair seat level for getting in bed and put higher to above their chair seat level for getting out of bed. Adjustable beds are also of great use in cases where the patient needs to be lifted into and out of bed by a third-party.

I was also allowed to give up the dubious delights involved with getting myself into and out of a car. I attempted getting into my physios saloon car on a few occasions but I couldn't even get my legs in properly let alone get my backside across the seemingly cavernous gap onto the seat. We tried using the 'sliding board' but it needed such a super human effort to get myself in that we eventually gave it up as defeating the purpose. However, I do know of two cases, without tricep control, who can get in and out and even drive a hand controlled car. But I do regard these cases as being freaks of their accidents, who I suspect are actually incomplete motor power cases, although they claim they are not.

I'm truly convinced that driving is out of the question for ninety per cent of c5/6 cases, although of course, if you can afford any amount of money to have a car suitably converted, there are c5 cases who would be able to drive. You do need to be lifted into and out of the car, which again defeats the whole concept of independence of being able to drive in the first place. Perhaps I shouldn't state here that driving is an impossibility for cases of my Level, since it might deter one or two would-be drivers from attempting to drive. As it is my sincere opinion I felt it should be set down in that light.

Whilst on the subject of cars, I'm pleased to be able to report that my brother David was now a proud car owner and could now take me out and about. It was now my opportunity to escape from the hospital at weekends when my brothers visited.

I would of course enjoy the traditional chicken sandwiches, prepared by good old Mum. I would then leap into David's car – only joking. I mean, after considerable effort on the part of my brothers and I, I would eventually be seated in the front seat of David's Ford Corsair and yes, we were soon under way.

Being the front seat passenger, I found myself in charge of the car radio cassette player and ' boy oh boy ' it was loud. My brothers understood that loud music helped me to deal with my paralysis and they were soon listening to some great rock music. I was a fan of groups, such as Black Sabbath, with the crazy Ozzie Osborne, Status Quo and Led Zeppelin. I must admit that we were rather naughty and would speed along the country lanes of Bedfordshire and Buckinghamshire, with me head banging to the music. Talking plainly, this was my moment of freedom, I couldn't shake my body, but I could certainly shake my head and that's exactly what I did. We also visited Dunstable Downs, Bedfordshire, where we would park up on top of the hill to watch the gliders dropping from the sky and eventually landing on grass at the bottom field. I particularly enjoyed watching the gliders being towed high into the sky by small aircraft.

Given the opportunity my brothers and I would also take part in a pint or two of beer at some of the wonderful pubs in the rural area. David was sensible of course and would usually have only one beer, due to the fact that he would be driving back to London later in the evening. There were time constraints which normally meant that I would be returned back to the hospital by 6pm. The duty orderly would be quick to return me to my bed, soon after which I would bid my brothers a safe journey home. I normally slept well after my adventures with my brothers. I very much appreciated their visits, bearing in mind the four hour return journey from Hackney to Stoke Mandeville. They both often worked five and a half day weeks and then gave up their Sunday off, to visit little old me!!

Within a week or two of getting out of bed most cases are introduced to 'standing' sessions. But, alas, this is not what it at first might appear to be, as all to many relatives of those concerned have discovered to their cost. The implication that the patient is well on the way to walking out of the hospital is just not so in ninety per cent of cases. The standing is brought about by artificial means in the shape of leg plaster cast supports, solely for the purpose of kidney drainage, improvement of circulation and prevention of early calcification of the bones in the trunk and legs through them not having any weight on them.

The plaster casts are made to fit the individual and your physio normally does the fitting. Only half a cast is made, built up against a stocking at the back of each leg from just below the rump to just above the ankles. During the moulding process great care is taken to keep the ankles free as if the cast were built around the ankle it would cause sores when being used during a standing session. At a later date you may need to have another set of plasters made in order to accommodate the thinness of the wasted legs. In my case the one set were good for a few years as my legs didn't waste.

When you first sit up after being in bed for so long, giddiness is experienced. This is due to the lower oxygen intake caused by the dropping diaphragm. A similar thing occurs when you stand for the first few times as the diaphragm drops lower still. For this reason it was thought that cervical cases were unable to endure the effects of standing up, this was in the early days of the spinal unit. Now, after the initial bouts of giddiness have been overcome, when standing for the first few times, most cervicals are able to stand without any ill effects. Putting the cast on the women presents no problems as the leg is simply straightened and the plaster is bandaged on securely down the length of the leg. However, with the males it is a little more difficult as the urine bag is strapped to a leg. To this end, new cases have zippers fitted up the inside of their trousers legs to enable the bag to be undone from whichever leg it is tied to and the plaster bandaged on before the "kipper" is replaced over the bandage and cast. The zipper is then done up again.

This is a necessity because the chap might pass water whilst stood up and should the drainage bag have been tightly held down under the bandages he would probably have become wet through as the water could not flow freely into the bag. At a later date, the unsightly zippers could be done away with as by then you have learnt to empty the bladder prior to standing, obviating the likelihood of ones passing whilst up, with the 'kipper' bandaged tightly to the leg under the trousers and plasters.

The actual standing, which has to be seen to be believed, is carried out by your physio (who is perhaps not over five foot four or so) who can manage to stand a fifteen stone, six footer without dropping him. Of course, not all the patients are big but a great many were as they were sportsmen. Your feet are positioned between the physios to prevent them sliding. Your arms are clasped around her neck (very enjoyable) if you can do this and the back of your trouser waist band is gripped by the physio. A good swing forward is then necessary to get your weight down onto your feet and then into a standing position. The hips have to be kept forwards of the trunk and feet once standing to prevent you from doubling up and sitting down again. With high lesions the trunk can sway in any direction and the hips can also sway all over the place. Once you are up and stood squarely there is very little weight on the physio as this is being carried down through your frame and plasters.

The physio usually finds it more comfortable to support her charge from behind during the fifteen minutes they are standing and she accordingly has to edge her way round to the back whilst ensuring the hips stay square and his trunk doesn't double over forwards. This happened to me on numerous occasions when I was being stood by a certain inexperienced young physio. You can easily double over and smash your face on your knees. Patients are usually stood between a set of two parallel bars with a full length mirror at one end to enable the physio and patient to see whether you are stood squarely. One might conclude that all it needed was for the patient to snatch a look, but this is not possible as any slight head movements cause the trunk to react and looking down would cause you to double up.

Again, you are presented with a dishevelled looking mess in the mirror....plasters on the legs, bowed body, bulging tummy, spotty face and messy hair....and to cap it all you are being held up by a woman half your size.

A standing session was considered to be necessary two or three times weekly, although I ended up standing once a week due to the difficulties involved with getting someone to do it. Constantly sitting allows debris to build up in the kidneys and therefore regular standing helps prevent this body waste material from forming into kidney stones. Urine can stagnate in the kidneys and bladder and standing also helps to drain this out.

The majority of cervical cases with tricep control are capable of supporting themselves safely between a set of parallel bars. They may occasionally allow their hips to sway a little to far backwards and double up. This is not to dangerous for them as they can prevent themselves from hitting their knees by hooking their arms over the bars. Although such cases still need supervision, as with my case, they are prone to being thrown off balance in any direction by their own involuntary muscular spasms. These spasms are usually more severe with back lesions but a good many physios are caught out and thrown over with their patient whenever a sudden set of spasms occur. The back cases developed them in their legs and the neck cases developed them in their legs and trunk, though less severely.

Many cases were able to move along between the bars by a method known as "swing through" . They lean forwards, taking the weight on their arms through the bars and as the weight comes off of their feet their legs "swing through". Eighteen inches to three feet can be gained with a single swing and they then re position their hands and swing through again. Of course this is not a practical means of getting about as it would necessitate having parallel bars everywhere but it is a good form of exercise in the bars.

However, some of the lowest cervicals are fit enough or I should say physically able enough to make use of the swing through method using a set of alloy crutches instead of the bars. This is an extremely strenuous means of getting about for any cervical and I am unaware of any cases who have adopted crutches as a permanent mode of getting around other than their wheelchairs.

For back cases, this is a practical method of getting about and they are issued with a set of lightweight leg calipers in place of the cumbersome plasters. The greater control over their trunk muscles enables them to keep better control over the sway of their hips and a good yard can be gained with each swing through, landing their feet nice and squarely with each cycle.

The calipers have a locking device at knee level to enable the user to sit down in their chair. The feet are held square by means of a small spring hooked onto the toe of the shoe from just above ankle level. They are not used as often as they might be because they are frowned upon as being rather unsightly. A wheelchair is now accepted in public but these calipers give the user a crippled look and they are not often used because of this.

There is however, an alternative to these calipers in the shape of a French invention which was developed in the states. It consists of an inflatable multi-tubular casing which is fitted around the paraplegics hips and legs and then zipped up the side. Unfortunately, this equipment is to bulky to be worn under trousers and there is nowhere an incontinent paraplegic can wear his urinal bag for free flow as its being worn inside would cause flow problems from the pressure caused by the inflated tubes.

The Circus.

Here, as might have been expected, all the patients performed. It was a weekly physio session held to show the doctors how the patients were progressing. As such a commotion was caused by everyone preparing to do their party tricks, perhaps the event had been aptly named as 'The Circus' Many of us felt like performing clowns and my first was nearly a disaster when I was about to undergo my balancing test. I looked around at the doctors and promptly lost balance, but my physio sat me up again and I was passed with a grunt and a nod from the head man himself.

On a subsequent occasion I was exhibited in my full glory, standing up in my leg plasters for my standing test. My physio had been in near panic stations over there not being a free set of parallel bars for us to use. When we finally gained a set and I was stood up, I recall how it seemed almost a non event with being over and done with so quickly. The fuss had been worthwhile though, as I had had another quick cuddle on the way up.

Mostly, the physio room seemed to be packed out. There were patients taking balancing and standing tests, numerous back lesions cases waiting to do a quick shuffle around on their leg calipers and crutches and an incomplete case or two about to show they were progressing towards eventually walking out of the hospital by their actually taking a few steps....whilst the remainder of us lesser mortals would sit back and watch in awe.

Finally, we would all be treated to a truly magnificent display of wheelchair gymnastics by those back cases who were able enough to get their wheelchairs up and down kerbs. To attain this particular feat they had to master the knack of balancing the wheelchair on its large back wheels. A push forward and a flick backwards would bring the chair to the required angle and the front wheels were then lowered onto the pavement, followed by a tug on the back wheels to bring the large wheels onto the pavement. To get down a kerb, the chair was again balanced at the required angle and the large wheels were then allowed to drop over the edge of the kerb whilst the chair was sitting tipped back. With much practice of this balancing art, the chairs could eventually be propelled at high speed whilst balanced on their large back wheels. Then getting up or down kerbs was frowned upon as being kids stuff, as going down a flight of steps was within the ability of the more able of these people. In fact, I once witnessed on American paraplegic negotiating an eight step flight.

However, it was all the more instructive in the circus if one of the novices happened to tip his chair to far backwards and come tumbling out as he could then demonstrate his ability in getting himself back into his chair. He had to position himself to be sat backwards onto the front of his chair. He then had to position his hands somehow on the chair behind him to be able to purchase enough of a lift to get his backside up to seat level.

Few cases were actually capable of achieving this feat as such a great effort is needed in the lift to overcome the height.

Archery and Table Tennis.

The physiotherapists held archery classes in the archery hall every afternoon. It turned out to be a very enjoyable pastime as well as a great form of exercise and rehabilitation. But, the questions were and still are, how does someone with no grip in the hands accomplish doing archery when they cannot even sit themselves up properly in a chair. These questions puzzled me and I was very eager to find out the answers. Cases of c5 and above couldn't do archery, at my level, aids were needed and cases with tricep control also had to resort to using a couple of aids, although, of course, the back cases could manage unaided.

All cervicals had to have the bow held into their hand and in the early days this was done with bandages. However, if a tight job was not obtained the accuracy of the archery was markedly reduced. There were often long faces whenever a new physio happened to tie a bow handle into ones palm to loosely. A tight fit could be had if one person held your fingers and thumb wrapped around the handle whilst another person attended to the bandaging. As there were usually six to eight cervicals to be done at once there was not enough time for two physios to be attending to one cervical.

The bow string was drawn by means of a hook which had to be bandaged into the other hand very well to withstand the pull of the bow (as much as forty pounds with some of the stronger bows). Cases without tricep control had to have a splint bandaged onto their bow arm to prevent their arm from bending under the strain of the draw. At my level the pull often caused me to lose a few inches of draw when my wrist was pulled inwards (due to not having control of my wrist flexer muscles), and I therefore had to have another small splint bandaged into place there.

All cervicals had to be harnessed into their chair to prevent them from falling off balance when an arrow was loosed and again, this was accomplished with bandages. A few times round my chest and under each arm etc., saw me almost ready to loose an arrow. I would frequently discover

I had had my shoulders tied back to tightly to allow me to get my hook arm across to meet my bow arm so the whole lot needed undoing and retying. There were a few harsh words uttered but I knew they enjoyed wasting their time with tying me up in bandages and anyway, it was all the more rewarding for them when I actually got a shot off and hit the correct target.

There were two chaps living in the hospital grounds who were excellent archers. They frequently entered competitions and they had therefore made all of the necessary securing equipment out of leather for ease and speed of it being fitted up. The leather strap used for the bow hand was held into place by buckles as was the leather strap for holding the hook. The arm splint which only one of them needed, was a piece of perspex, again held into place with buckles, The harnesses were slipped over their head, with one chap needing a single shoulder support and the other (without triceps) needing a double. They often practised when I was in the hall and they could be fitted up in a matter of two or three minutes as opposed to my ten or more.

The wheelchairs were positioned sideways on to the targets in a line across the hall. The cardinal rule was that no patient should have an arrow in a bow whenever a member of staff happened to be between the wheelchairs and targets. An arrow could travel at up to two hundred miles an hour when the bow had been fully drawn and could therefore go straight through a body. Whilst the arrows were being loosed in every direction but the correct one with us novices, it was a very brave physio who ventured down the hall to retrieve any spent arrows in the knowledge that one of us clots might have another arrow notched.

Numerous arrows were temporarily irretrievable as they had been shot off into the roof during attempts at loading. I confess to having done this on many an occasion as there was only one way I could load my bow successfully. The arrows were laid out across my chair arms and both hands being in bandages necessitated my notching an arrow and then hooking the bow string. I then had to draw the bow and raise my arms and head as I came up to face the target. The hook would often slip off of the string first and the arrow was shot off in whichever direction it happened to be pointing at the time.

As with anything I concentrated on my sweating output increased the very moment I

started "popping off" with a few arrows and I had
to be mopped up every few minutes with paper
towels brought from a nearby loo. It was then that I
began wearing a towel permanently around my
neck, but it and my clothes became soaked
through, when again I had to go and get changed
before going off to physio or O T. I never did
become a competent archer, probably due to
laziness. After a few months my fear of sweating yet
more profusely than I was doing, just to let fly with
a few arrows, increasingly kept me away from
archery classes. Eventually, when I did attend, it
was as a spectator only.

The table tennis sessions turned out to be a
very similar kettle of fish, at least as far as I was
concerned. There wasn't quite such a rigmarole
with being fitted up as all that was necessary was
for the bat to be bandaged into my hand and the
shoulders to be secured to the chair back handles.
But, yet again the sweat poured out of me and the
resultant tenseness around the neck and shoulders
made it very difficult to serve and play the strokes
without being very uncomfortable at each and
every move. However, as a poor craftsman blames
his tools, so, a rather pathetic specimen of a
quadriplegic can bow to the reader in the

knowledge that the dreaded sweat can be blamed for my being a poor contestant at archery and table tennis.

Old Patients.

Many of the patients on my new ward were classed as old patients because of the number of years it had been since their respective accidents had occurred. The reasons for them having to return for treatment were numerous and I think there were not more than perhaps, two or three cases at a time for a similar reason in attending.

Pressure sore cases seemed to be predominant and having seen some of these large ulcerated and infected sores, it amazes me as to how and why these people allowed the sores to develop into such a deteriorated state in the first place. If a sore place or a bruise is discovered it should be treated with respect for the impending menace that it is and you need to retire to bed for a week or two until it has healed. It should not be continually sat or layed upon until it ulcerates, resulting in one having to spend up to six months in bed.

It appeared that many of these cases that I met during the months to come, had become generally depressed with their lives outside of the hospital and had deliberately allowed their pressure sores to develop to the state whereby they could be readmitted to Stoke for a carefree few months in bed. When this negative attitude of these patients first dawned on me, it made me rather frightened at the prospect of my having to return home sometime when I might well adopt the same frame of mind that these people had done. But, perhaps a big relative point in favour of their wanting a six months hideaway in bed was down to the fact that they had been chair-bound for ten, twenty or even thirty years.

Still, I asked my physio for her opinion as to why these people had developed such severe sores and she stated that she thought they were developed by sheer carelessness and a great deal of self neglect. Most sores were around the hips, buttocks or lower back. It was apparent that they must have been started with a bruise from a knock of some kind. A paraplegic might be getting in and out of a car several times daily catching their hips and backside virtually every time and not being able to feel this or caring about it either. He/she would sit on the bruises until they eventually broke down into sores.

Probably, a number of these cases will be reacting angrily over my stating that these sores are developed due to carelessness and self neglect and I do acknowledge that many cases can develop sores even though they try everything to prevent their development. Thin people can continually develop sores and people that received wounds at the time of their accident can have the wound develop into a pressure sore which continually breaks down.

A major place for a sore to develop is at the base of the spine, When in the sitting position the coccyx is pointing directly into the chair cushion, exerting a great deal of pressure to that area of skin which has very little flesh for padding. The pointed bone causes bruising and the skin is eventually broken through and when this happens it is very difficult to prevent it recurring. The haunches of the backside can also break through the skin, especially with thin people, again, causing great difficulty with preventing their recurrently breaking through.

Once the haunches or base of the spine has broken through a few times, the doctor will probably attempt to remedy the trouble by operating. They will chip away part of the offending bone in the hope that once the wound has healed that will be the end of it. But, sad to say, this is a poor means of dealing with the problem. I know a man who continually had to return to have more bone chipped away as his coccyx broke through again and again.

Incidentally, the majority of patients cannot feel any pain from their body area below their lesion level and therefore no anaesthetic is used during such operations. I recall telling a chap who was about to go to the theatre for one of these ops that I would be sick at the thoughts of just lying there wide awake whilst they were chipping away at my bone. He grinned all over his face and told me that there was nothing to it after you had been through it a few times. He informed me that some people do experience severe headaches during the op but then a quick injection puts them out if it becomes too unbearable. He had evidently developed a philosophical frame of mind towards the whole subject.

I know of one person who actually died whilst in Stoke with sores, but this wasn't as a direct result of his sores, but rather because he gave up the will to live. He was in his early thirties, he had an attractive young wife and four beautiful young children. He had developed the attitude that he had let his family down as they were having to live on Social Security and he was forever reproaching himself for having been silly enough to break his neck. His life had been completely shattered in his view and he wanted no further part of it. He ate very little and was eventually placed on an intravenous drip. Shortly after, he was moved to another ward (when ours was being redecorated) and passed away.

Being eighteen at the time, his seemingly needless death really got through to me. But, during the two years and two months that I was in the hospital, I was to see a great deal of that sort of thing and my general attitude towards such incidents was to become increasingly hardened.

Apart from the general influx of pressure sore cases, there were and no doubt still are, many, many cases being readmitted for bladder and/or kidney troubles. Paralysed people are very prone to developing water infections, which can infect the bladder or kidneys or both. When an infection is severe it can cause heavy bleeding. Pain cannot be felt and so the first thing you know about it is when heavy sweating suddenly breaks out and your water turns dark red and bubbly looking.

With a mild infection your G P can prescribe a course of antibiotic tablets but with a severe infection you may need to go into hospital (preferable a spinal unit where they have the medical know-how to cope), to undergo a course of antibiotic injections. When an infection is severe it is usually accompanied by heavy vomiting and orally administered antibiotic tablets cannot be kept down.

After I had been discharged from Stoke to my home I had the misfortune of developing such a severe infection and was admitted to a small country hospital as the beds at Stoke were all full. Well, the doctors there could not cope and I later went into a coma for eight hours. The doctors didn't expect me to recover. In my view, this near fatal situation was brought about because the doctors dealing with my case thought it below there professional dignity to ring Stoke and ask for advice as to the most advisable treatment for me. Furthermore, when my frantic relatives contacted

Stoke to ask them what could be done, they were told that it was not medically ethical for the doctors at Stoke to advise the doctors at my hospital over how to treat me.

More troublesome than infections is the development of bladder or kidney stones. If these are small enough they can be flushed out by the patient drinking copious quantities of fluids. Larger stones have to be removed by operation, although the doctors are rather averse to this course of action until it becomes absolutely necessary.

A third alternative is available (for removing stones from all people and not just those who are paralysed), in the form of introducing a pliant lead into the bladder and up into the kidneys -by literally watching to see when the lead has reached the stone via a 'picture' being transmitted to a screen by a complicated x-raying technique. A small electric shock is then transmitted to an electrode at the tip of the probe shattering the stone in the process. A few attempts are sometimes necessary, but once the stone has been broken up it can be washed out by the patient drinking large quantities of fluids.

With all this wear and tear being caused to the kidneys from infections and stones, it is no wonder that the kidneys can eventually cease functioning over the years. (renal failure being the main cause of para' and quadriplegics' deaths). I met many patients who had already lost a kidney.. or who were in hospital to have one removed. Their main worry seemed to be as to what their situation would be when they lost the other one??

Well, we are all that there is a waiting list of people awaiting kidney transplants, who are most probably being kept alive on kidney dialysis machines. There are a limited number of these machines and a team of doctors therefore have to decide which patients are to be allowed the limited amount of time available on any given machine. The criteria used for their granting someone life or death is based upon the individuals value to the community. Therefore, as the majority of paralysed people do not work, they will probably be given a 'thumbs down' as they will not be considered to be 'contributing citizens'. When my kidneys temporarily ceased functioning, kidney dialysis machines, or a kidney transplant op', were not even considered. It appeared to be very much the case that an 'incurable' should be allowed to 'bow out' quietly.

Several cases were admitted to have what was known as 'spinal blocks'. These were carried out on back cases who happened to be suffering from severe leg muscle spasms and the 'blocking' was simply a means by which the spasms can be markedly reduced or prevented from occurring altogether.

Pure alcohol is injected into the base of the spine, usually causing the spasms to cease. However, this method of dealing with the problem was not considered to be a good means of control as the injecting of the alcohol was considered to be somewhat akin to playing with fire. But, this method was only used on cases where drugs were of no use and if a first injection didn't do the trick, a second dose was administered with reluctance.

The doctor often demonstrated this treatment to be effective, yet apparently, they didn't know just how or why it had the effect that it did. But, as with electric shock therapy, which is currently being used as a 'god-given' panacea throughout our mental hospitals. It is seen to be effective, and therefore it is readily used.

Both 'old' and 'new' patients are prone to undergoing a fearful experience known as a 'flare-up' – a condition thought to be brought about by a patients having been in the sun to long. I have undergone a few of these flare-ups over the years and you feel as if you are about to pass on to the happy hunting grounds at the time. The condition lasts for approximately forty-eight hours and it is characterised by, a high temperature, dirty water, profuse sweating, shivering, headaches and sometimes vomiting as well.

It doesn't come on until seven or eight hours after you have been out in the sun. When it hits a 'new' case during the middle of the night, a state of near panic ensue with ones relatives wondering what it is all about An old hand knows that he just has to weather the storm and therefore it is not really imperative for one to return to hospital.

As great a quantity of fluids should be consumed to keep the temperature down and to prevent dehydration. A fan could also be used to keep the person cool, although this should be switched off if the shivering becomes to great.

If you wish to avoid developing a 'flare-up' a hat should be worn when you are out in the sun. I disliked doing this as it defeats the purpose of sunning one's self. I never wore a hat, though, woe is me when I do develop a flare-up. The main contributing feature seems to be in getting to much sun on the back of the head and neck. If you avoid doing this it will cut down the risks of developing a flare-up.

Incidentally, I know one paraplegic who died whilst in the throes of a fare-up, although it wasn't the flare up which caused his death. He had been in the chair for some twelve years or so, and he had become generally despondent, He wasn't eating much when he developed the flare-up and with the weakness and depression he just didn't pull through.

Every day of the week there are patients arriving for their annual check-up. These are mainly carried out to keep an eye on the patients after discharge. They also provide the hospital with a ready flow of mass data as to the effects that time is having on the patients. A general physical check is carried out, similar to the one that is given when you first enter the spinal unit. Any changes in your condition are noted. A blood sample is taken, a sterile water sample is taken to be checked for infections and the rectum is checked for cuts or growths.

A series of x-rays are taken, known as I.V.P., or intravenous pilogramme. This is to ensure that the kidneys and bladder are free of stones. This is done by means of a dye being injected intravenously, usually into your arm, from where it is cleared out of the blood stream by the kidneys, dying them and the bladder etc., on its way out of the body. When the dye has had time to get through the x-rays are taken and any stones present will then be shown up on the shots.

The actual injection of the dye is relatively painless but some patients react adversely to the dye itself and some are even sick. Many years ago, when this type of x-raying technique was being developed, numerous patients experienced adverse effects from the various types of dye which were being experimented with. This is a rare occurrence now as a suitable type of dye has been found. The only casualties are usually found amongst the squeamish patients who cannot stand having injections.

If the x-rays are clear the patient is allowed to return home on the same day. If stones are present you may be allocated a bed or be asked to return at a later date when a bed becomes available. The results of the water test are forwarded to your GP a

few days later. If you have a mild infection the GP
will issue a course of antibiotics or alternatively you
may be asked to return to Stoke for treatment.

The Paraplegic Games.

I was lucky enough to be present at Stoke
Mandeville in a year which coincided with Great
Britain's being the host nation for the games.
Teams from such far away places as Australia,
Japan, Canada, America and South America were
competing and the friendly atmosphere of a major
international competition could be felt in the air.

At the time the success of the games
depended very much upon the clemency of the
weather, as most of the events were held out in a
field at the rear of the hospital grounds. Since that
time a wonderful sports stadium has been built and
the games can now be held without fear of a
sudden cloudburst ruining them.

Naturally enough not all the events normally
held at an athletics meeting could be carried out as
the competitors were all chair-bound. A great many
were still held and it was impossible to get around
to see everything.

The major competitions were, Basket Ball, Swimming, Archery, Fencing and Table Tennis. Although people competing in other events may have considered theirs to be the major of the games, it was these events which were the more spectacular and which consequently drew the largest crowds.

The swimming competition is fascinating to watch as it is very interesting to discover just how different levels of paralysed people do manage to swim. However, I believe there are numerous good swimmers who are reluctant to enter into any public competitions as this involves displaying their dropped stomach in full view. I must confess to being in this reluctant category, although the size of my stomach is probably due to the large quantity of wine and lager which passes through it. But, I would still be ineligible for a gala anyway as my standard of swimming is still rather pathetic.

The distances raced are much less than those raced at an ordinary gala as the contestants can only use their arms (although there is an exception to this apparent rule which I shall mention a little later).

One of the men I saw in a two lengths front crawl race (approximately forty yards) had everyone worried because he didn't lift his head to take a breath. But it was later discovered he was a c5/6 case who couldn't actually lift his head clear of the water to take a breath until the race was finished. He could then use the side of the pool wall to hook his arms into for leverage. He must have had the most efficient lungs I have ever known for a man of his level. He was clearly a born swimmer as he could still swim like a fish even though he was at possibly the highest level at which a neck case is still capable of swimming.

The three group categories for the races were, back cases, tricep cervicals and non tricep cervicals. Yet, the thing wrong with this grouping system was that there was no provision in the rules to prevent 'incomplete' cases race against 'complete' cases. Some of the 'incomplete' motor power cases could use their legs to propel themselves. They therefore had a great advantage over the 'complete' motor power cases they raced against. In fact, I once saw a man swimming against complete back cases, who was actually able to walk. He had broken his back at sometime, in the past and he had caused very little damage to his spinal chord resulting in very little paralysis. However, he was classed as an 'incomplete' back case andhe could therefore enter competitions against 'complete' cases of his level.

Of course, very few 'incomplete' cases are as marked in their greater physical abilities as this man was. Even where a few muscles can be used, the advantage over a 'complete' case is wrong. The games committee should amend the rules to rule out "incomplete' motor power cases racing against the 'completes'.

Other Unfortunates.

During one particularly long period of illness for which I was confined to bed, I was moved up the ward to be nearer the TV and I consequently made many more friends. Oddly enough, I was beginning to be regarded as part of the furniture by that time since there were cases returning to our ward who had been discharged perhaps some six to eight months previously. One man who returned again and again for kidney troubles, a Liverpudlian by birth, was often very ill, but he always had me near to hysterics with his rye sense of humour. He had sustained a broken neck some twelve years previously when he and some friends were involved in a car crash when returning to their army barracks after having been out on the beer. He considered himself to be a prematurely retired gentleman of independent means. But, the fact was that the army had no facilities for looking after a quadriplegic private and he had been pensioned off on full pay for life.

Yet, herein, lies an anomaly, which I shall deal with more fully in a later chapter, concerning the point that some people sustain their injury under favourable circumstances and are duly compensated, whereas others sustain their injury at a bad time or pace and receive no compensation whatsoever.

Another quadriplegic, whom I later became good friends with, was renowned throughout the hospital, at the time, for the spectacular way in which he had sustained his injury. He had been driving home very late one night, after having worked a double shift, when he nodded off at the wheel and his car careered straight through the high street shop window of a record retailers....setting him up as being the record holder for having smashed the most records in the world.

His injury was at c5/6 and he was the man who had
to have a set of ramps built up to his front door. He
had a wife, kids and a mortgage and all he could do
was joke about the way he had been half killing
himself with work in the 'rat race', which now
seemed so futile. He did manage to hold onto his
house, though I don't know where the mortgage
money came from and the accident brought him
and his family very close together.

He was much better than me at pushing his
chair, but we often used to laugh at the bloody
pathetic rate we made any headway going up any
slight hill. Because of this, free wheeling downhill
was very enjoyable for us and every morning he
would leave the ward grinning in anticipation of
the roll down the hospital hills. One morning
however, he was rolling down one of the steeper
hills on his way to the lower physio department,
when his chair hit a radiator and catapulted him
out of his chair at high speed. He hadn't learnt to
keep an arm hooked behind his chair back at that
time and although he was brought back into the
ward on a stretcher, he was up and about again that
afternoon.

One of his great regrets was, no longer being
able to tour the London pubs, playing the piano

and singing. He could however, still down a pint and sing to himself, so things weren't as bad as they might have been. He took up painting after he was discharged, with the brushes being held, woven between his fingers and I understand that he has become a successful painter. We do attend the same holiday centre each year, but, as yet, I have not been booked up whenever he was there. Still, maybe I will run into him one day.

I was moved into the ward annex on one occasion. In the opposite bed was a mere gnome of a man from Norfolk. He had been a farmer and he and his relatives had the funniest accent that I have Ever heard. He made me laugh every time he spoke. He was sixty at the time and he had sustained a broken neck. How had is happened? Well, this inoffensive little man had apparently been trying to prevent a bull from mating with a cow, when, having somehow gotten caught in-between the two he managed to break his neck. They say love conquers all, and it had certainly conquered him. However, whether the pair then mated, whilst he lay paralysed on the grass, the old man wouldn't say, but I suspect they did!

After I had been in hospital for about twenty months, I made friends with a welsh lad of twenty four, who had sustained his injury playing rugby whilst in the Navy. He hit his head on another mans hip bone when doing a hard flying tackle, breaking his neck. His level was c6/7, but he was lucky, in a way, as his was an 'incomplete' motor power break. He had some grip in his hands, (he could pick up a pint without a handle) and he had some leg muscle control. I don't believe his leg muscle control was developed to the point where he could stand, but, such movement is definitely an asset when being dressed as he could raise his hips to the point whereas his trousers and pants could be pulled up easily by a third party.

It is a tedious job to dress a paralysed person, what with getting the trousers well up around the waist etc., and any help from the person is very helpful. Therefore, I mention this point, because although this man wouldn't have thought his muscle control to be much use, since he couldn't stand up, any muscle movement can be put to good use, even though it may at first appear to be of complete insignificance to the person concerned.

I met two other man who had sustained their neck injuries playing rugby. One was somewhat of a celebrity (although I had never heard of him), an All-England International, named Danny Hearn.

He had broken his neck in exactly the same way as the sailor had done. And he was also an 'incomplete' motor power break. He could stand, unaided and he eventually progressed to walking a few steps after the bruising to his spinal cord had gone completely down. He could dress himself, get on and off a bed, on and off a toilet and in and out of a car, all due to the fact that he was 'incomplete' to the extent of him being able to stand up and sit down with a little effort and concentration.

I mention this man, however, because he was used as a 'show-piece' by the hospital physio staff, who showed him off to crowds of medical visitors as being a wonder of modern day medicine. They showed him off as having been a compete motor case, who had been healed by the hospital staff, when these people were not made aware that he had been an incomplete case in the first place. I also witnessed this sort of exhibition going on when an incomplete motor power policeman we shown off. Who had only been left paralysed in the arms and hands. He had sustained a broken neck, but here he was walking about and the visitors were under the impression that he had been a complete motor case, when he had in fact, been an incomplete from the start.

I am not however, trying to show up the
hospital as being a 'con' as the saying goes, since I
am well aware that many great achievements are
brought about there, to say the least. But, this
impression conveyed to the visitors, that the place
was a dream factory in which paralysed people are
brought in and fit people walk out was decidedly
wrong. I am only aware of two instances where this
type of exhibition was done, but if it is done to
enhance the reputation of the unit, it should be
stopped.

The second Rugby case was a very severe case
of paralysis indeed who was not shown off other
than in the light that he was the only living c2/3
case in the world. He was completely paralysed
apart from minute head movements. He was
virtually always connected up to a respirator via a
trachea tube inserted into his throat. He could
speak in whispers, if the air-hole was momentarily
blocked off to allow some air to activate his vocal
chords. But, with the hole open the air was not
allowed to get high enough for him to speak. It was
claimed that he would be able to come off of the
respirator for up to two or three hours at a stretch
sometime in the future and as he was able to blow
and suck enough to operate the POSSUM machine,

at that time, although only extremely slowly, I would imagine he'd have acquired one after having been discharged.

One of the unluckiest cases I ever met (that is apart from considering all cases to have been unlucky), was a young woman who had been a nurse prior to her mishap. The reason I consider her to have been particularly unlucky was because she had sustained a 'complete' motor power neck lesion whilst sitting in an armchair. She had dropped off to sleep and she didn't know whether she had broken her neck whilst sleeping or by jerking it at an awkward angle when she awoke. But, whichever way it happened, the fact remains, she broke her neck without ever having left her armchair.

A spinal injury can be sustained by anyone under virtually any set of accidental circumstances imaginable. Yet, to have become paralysed in such a way as this, must surely leave one to conclude that it was caused by the hand of fate. She was another c5/6complete lesion (how numerous we were) and she was a beautiful blond with a wonderful smile. She had lost a great deal, but she was still smiling, having accepted her lot as readily as anyone could have.

Sex

The hospital staff eventually decided I shouldn't be allowed to occupy a much needed ward bed unnecessarily and I was accordingly moved out to a place in the hospital grounds known as the hostel. Here, I was allocated a single room and at a later date I began courting a certain young lady.

Well, naturally enough, my thoughts turned increasingly to the subject of sex. It was around this time that I was first seriously concerned with the problems of sex for the paralysed. Sexual worries can present quite a headache when one gets around to wondering about 'Can I' or 'Cant I' and whether one is actually single or married, the problems encountered by the individual are much the same.

For men, the first question that arises is whether or not one can get an erection. Well, in the early post accident days this ability is usually lost completely, although, it does return later on. There are two ways in which an erection can be caused, either psychologically, by one having sexy thoughts....reading sexy literature or looking at sexy photographs etc. or by directly stimulating the genital area, causing the penis to become erect by a virtual reflex action. The first can be had by 'incomplete' cases, as their brain can cause an erection by sending messages down to the genital area; and the latter can be had by 'complete' cases, as this reflex action can be brought about without there being any messages received from the brain.

Its unlikely that one will be able to ejaculate as the nerves which carried the messages to trigger an ejaculation will probably have been injured, but of course, if one happens to be an 'incomplete' lesion the chances of being able to ejaculate are increased with the greater incompleteness the lesion happens to be.

Even if one can ejaculate, very few 'para' and quadriplegics can father children as their sperm count is usually to low. However, a couple might wish to consider the possibility of having a child via the 'A.I.D' organisation. This stands for artificial insemination by donor and as the name implies, the semen is supplied by an anonymous third party, who has been rigorously vetted and who is never informed as to with which woman he has fathered the child. Of course, the moral question concerning such a concept is very much open to discussion between the couple involved, but, anyone deciding on taking this step should contact their GP for the address of the 'A.I.D' organisation.

On the whole, as might have been expected, the fit partner will be the dominant person during intercourse; and as far as orgasm is concerned, this again depends very much on the 'complete' or 'incompleteness 'of one lesion. A 'complete' case may be unable to feel anything at all and an 'incomplete' case will have various amounts of feeling depending on how 'incomplete' he is; but there is a great variation between the two extremes of a 'complete' and 'incomplete' case.

Most cases are incontinent in the bladder and therefore the bladder should be expressed prior to attempting intercourse, as this not only obviates the likelihood of ones passing at an undesirable moment. It also helps to prevent the loss of an erection as this is what happens when one passes water. If a condom is being worn, this can easily be slipped off and if you have an indwelling catheter, this can either be removed or a condom can be put over the penis and catheter together.

For women, sex presents much less of a problem, as, on the whole, female sexual function is largely unaffected. As with men, however, the annoying part comes with ones being a complete or incomplete lesion as this governs whether or not you will be able to experience an orgasm. Again, a complete case will not be able to feel anything, whereas an incomplete case may be able to feel enjoyment to varying extents. The bladder should be emptied first and if a catheter is being used it can be removed or taped to your stomach.

Having conceived, there is no reason why a paralysed woman shouldn't give birth to a normal healthy child. However, if you are injured during pregnancy you may give birth rather early, especially if your lesion is a high back or neck level. Loss of periods may be experienced during early post accident days, but they usually return to normal after a few months. The higher lesions may have some difficulty with the birth, due to their not having any muscular control in the lower trunk etc., but it is only rarely that a caesarean operation is necessary.

Of course, it may be that a couple do not wish to have a child and in this case the normal methods of contraception can be employed, i.e. a condom, withdrawal or a vasectomy operation for males; a coil, a cap, the pill, a loop or sterilisation, for females. On the other hand, however, if a couple cannot have a child of their own they might do well to consider the merits of adoption.

As I have said, the sexual problems encountered by a couple with one of the two being, or becoming paralysed can present a few headaches; but with a little knowledge and intelligence the difficulties can be overcome. Naturally, my being a layman, I'm not qualified to go into the subject at any greater depth, but, the above information will be of use to those whom it concerns and I've no doubt that the doctors at Stoke Mandeville Hospital will prove to be somewhat more than obliging to anyone requesting more detailed information related to the subject.

The Hostel; Ward 3; Discharge.

After I had been a hostel resident for a few weeks my dark forebodings about the place had been largely dispelled as it turned out to be a reasonable place to live in. It was managed by a charge nurse and his wife (an ex-ward sister) and any difficult medical problems were referred to the hospital doctors as the hostel residents were still officially under their care, although the hostel was a distinctly separate building.

You could push over to the main buildings for some physiotherapy or O.T or if you wished you could just wait until a physio was appointed to visit the hostel to carry out the necessary standing sessions. However, many of the twenty or so residents were absolutely fed up with this weekly standing routine and it was often necessary for the physio to hunt them down and convince them that a stand was a necessity for the continued good health of their kidneys etc.

The building had originally been opened to cater for short stay cases, but it was apparent that many of the people had settled themselves in to the extent that they hadn't the slightest thoughts of their ever being moved out. They either didn't have reliable friends or relatives outside with whom they could live, or they had decided to remain in the hostel as a defiant gesture of independence and in either case the hostel was as good a place to live as any other institution. There was nothing laid on officially to occupy the residents, which made the days drag by, even though I was gotten up last and put back to bed first, since the orderlies considered the others had priority over me, being a newcomer. A book could be read or a game of chess could occasionally be arranged but these pastimes had the effect of making you become rather withdrawn and introverted. There was a regular card school, but this was a closed shop to everyone but the foursome who were used to playing bridge together.

An adjoining workshop was open for some of the residents to while away a few hours each day with the assembling of electrical circuits and the like. This work was a little beyond the cervical cases as they didn't have any finger movement. A suitable form of work was always being sough for the cervicals, but nobody knew what kind of work was needed and consequently any type of work which was brought in was frequently found to be so basic it was soul destroying.

I was only expected to be in the hostel for a few months, until such time as my home had been converted and I therefore avoided doing any of the work as I considered that it might appear I was taking some of the earning capacity away from the

long term residents who needed the cash. They
were treated in much the same way as people in
other institutions throughout the country, in so far
as they were given, at that time, 'eighteen shillings'
per week in the workshop, as of right by the state;
yet. if an industrious individual happened to earn
more than 'two pounds' per week in the workshop,
the excess amount was automatically deducted
from his eighteen shillings per week allowance, by
the Social Security office concerned. So there was
actually very little incentive for anyone to work,
although some of them put up with this near slave
labour and they put in virtually a full working week
in order to earn their maximum amount allowable,
a measly two pounds.

I soon discovered that the rigours of a hard
push back over to the hospital was infinitely
preferable to the boredom in the hostel, although,
the push over was made particularly precarious by
there being a short, sharp hill, just outside the
workshop doors which necessarily had to be
negotiated. There was a lawn at the bottom of the
hill and as my chair tended to accelerate out of
control, the brake had to be applied and released at
the precise moments necessary in order to avoid

the chair running onto the lawn and tipping me out.

This hill was made to be downright dangerous for cervicals to negotiate a few months later as some construction workers had opened up a six foot trench for laying some sewerage pipes and this bloody great hole had been petitioned off by means of one single rope. Well, one evening I was attempting to push my chair back up the hill to get back into the workshop doors, when my wheels slipped out of my control straight towards the trench, ending up with me perched over the hole, being held from going down into the muddy water by a single rope and there wasn't a soul about. My shouts for help went unheard until an orderly returning to his quarters happened by. All I could do was laugh the experience off, but it had been extremely nerve wrecking being poised there over a hole. Yet, I wasn't involved in the campaign to get it filled in as a setback caused me to be returned to the main hospital building.

Ward 3.

I had been at home for a weekend when my
sweating output suddenly increased and I assumed
I was in for a dreaded flare-up. At the hostel the
charge nurse thought I was having a flare-up and I
accordingly had to sweat it out until a doctor
arrived to examine me on the Monday morning. It
was his opinion that something had upset my
kidneys. He accused me of having been drinking
the forbidden hard spirits over the weekend and
since I couldn't deny I had had a few, I was harshly
condemned as being my own worst enemy.
However, he decided to do a manual bowel check
and when he rolled me over he was confronted
with a large abscess which had just burst open on
my backside. We were all relieved to have
discovered the cause of my dire situation and I was
accordingly shipped off to Ward 3 that afternoon.

The doctor decided to cut the abscess open
and this act necessitated my spending the
following three months in bed, being turned side
to side every four hours to enable my backside to
heal. After a couple of weeks, my Welsh friend
reported he was being discharged and as I knew
very few people on the ward this contributed to my
developing a rather severe state of depression.
Nevertheless, being a misery did nobody any good,

not least of all myself and after awhile I managed to snap out of it and I then made many more friends amongst the staff and patients.

It was on this ward that it was brought home to me again as to the thousand and one ways in which a spinal injury can be sustained. It is an accepted fact that the building and construction industry has the highest accident rate figures throughout all industry, but, for some uncanny reason it had never occurred to me that these figures constituted accidents involving anything more serious than the odd cut finger or bruised hand etc. Yet, here, on one ward, in one hospital, at any given time, were three cases of the severely paralysed, sustained whilst working on building sites.

One chap at the far end of the ward, had fallen backwards off of a scaffolding board, breaking his back (at c4 as I recall) when landing on a pile of debris. One, a few beds away had fallen off of an extension ladder, breaking his neck when he landed on his head. The third chap, perhaps the unluckiest of the trio, had sustained a broken neck when some clot had dropped a full box of tools on his head from three floors up. Apparently, he would have been dead but for the fact that he was wearing a safety helmet. He broke his neck instead of getting his skull smashed in.

There were the expected car crash cases (usually cervical injuries as a result of whiplash or hitting the windscreen), the ex sporting fraternity, the motorbike ton-up boys, and of course the usual batch from the domestic accidents category.

A chap from this last group had sustained a neck lesion when falling off of a set of step ladders whilst doing a spot of, do it yourself. (he certainly had done it for himself). He was a managing director of an international paper making firm and he just couldn't figure out why such a decent hard working bloke as himself, had been singled out for such a fate.

There was a young lad in a bed near the entrance to the ward who had my heartfelt sympathy as he was a fellow sweat case. He could put up with the paralysis he said, if only the damned sweat would stop oozing out of him. It was clearly getting him down, more so I believe, because he often claimed that he was the only one who had to endure it. Even though I frequently ensured him that I too was a sweat case, he didn't believe me, until, I was later gotten out of bed to prevent my sweating self to him. He was pleased to hear that there was a two year time limit to his having to endure the sweating and I was pleased to note that his sweating was more profuse than mine. Well, I managed to have a couple of games of chess with him and about a fortnight after I had been up, I was shipped back over to the hostel.

Discharged.

My single room had been given to one of the young women and I was squared away in a corner bed in a four bed room. In the bed next to mine was another young chap...who informed me that I was sleeping in a dead mans bed and in the other two beds were a couple of old men. These two were always tucked up by seven every night, after-which, my friend and I were reprimanded as being 'noisy young bastards' whenever we made the slightest sound. They were absolutely averse to any kind of music being played and we therefore had to fit our music sessions in when this pair were fast asleep after lunch at the dining room table. The situation could so easily have been remedied if the charge nurse had changed a few beds around and put us youngsters in with other youngsters, but it was futile to persist in asking him to do this, and now whenever I hear of cases in which young disabled people have been placed in hospital geriatric wards, my heart goes out to them.

Apart from my room situation, things were beginning to look up at around this time as my sweating was definitely easing off and I was getting out and about a little more frequently. Late passes could be obtained from the charge nurse on request (to be endorsed by a doctor) and I was taking frequent advantage of this splendid facility in arranging for pushers(preferably by the fairer sex, but not essentially so) to take me to our local pub. By this time, the orderlies had accepted me as being an old hand and I could often stay out until midnight without getting into to much hot water when I returned in a rather inebriated state. Whenever I couldn't get a late pass(as they didn't allow to many cervicals out in one night) or a pusher, I would wheel my chair over to the wards for a card session with the ever present card sharks, in the hope of being able to pick up a 'few bob' to finance my next forage out to the pub.

On one such evening, I was returning to the hostel rather late when I had a rather harrowing experience. A short cut could be had back to the hostel by passing through a set of French doors just outside of which was a small hill leading onto a concrete path. The path turned right at about ninety degrees....there were flower beds on either side of it....it we only just wide enough to take the width of a wheelchair. Well, in order to steer the chair successfully down the hill and around the path the right brake has to be applied and released at precise moments, only this night it was raining.

A friend who was returning to the hostel with me, managed to steer his chair down and around okay, he was a case who had triceps control, But, when I applied my brake at the usual precise moment, I had forgotten to account for the wet surface and my chair careered over the edge of the path tipping me head first into the freshly turned, very muddy flower beds. I attempted to break my fall by putting my arms out....which was a vain effort, as not having triceps they just folded up on impact. My feet had been strapped onto the foot-plates and the chair had therefore been brought over on top of me. My head, arms and knees were sunk into the earth, several inches deep and my 'friend' just sat there in the rain, laughing hysterically for what seemed an eternity, because as he later explained, it appeared that I was still sitting squarely in my chair, only upside down!!!

When he finally gained control of himself he realised he couldn't get past my chair to get back into the hospital for help. He then took another twenty minutes in getting in through another entrance about two hundred yards away. By that time I was completely soaked through and after three people had finally managed to get me out of the flower bed and back into my chair I was given a push back to the hostel. The orderlies then decided it was time for them to 'play games' when they made out they were to busy to put me to bed, and anyway, as I always wanted to go to bed late, there was no reason they should put me to bed early that night either. They then put me to bed over an hour later and it was lucky I didn't develop pneumonia through being in wet clothes for so long.

PART THREE.

Hospital Discharge.

Well, January slipped by and I was informed
that our home adapting operations were nearing a
point whereby I should soon be allowed to go
home. At the end of March I was given the 'green
light' and discharged, leaving Stoke Mandeville,
two years and two months after my accident to the
very day. I decided my brother David would have
the pleasure of driving me home in his recently
acquired Ford corsair. The car was of course packed
to the gunnel's and you will be pleased to hear, that
I'm sparing you the finer details. The corsair was a
reasonably large car, which would afford me a
comfortable ride home. I noted that David had
been smoking in the car, prior to his arrival at the
hospital. I never commented of course, because '
beggars cannot be choosers '.

As we drove further and further away from
Stoke, my feelings at leaving the place were
decidedly mixed. In one respect I was very pleased
to be leaving as I knew I would be treated as a
human being at home as opposed to being treated
like a carcass of meat by the orderlies. But, in
another respect I was experiencing a certain degree
of remorse at leaving the place in which I had

experienced so much. It had by no means been a pleasant period in my life, nor had it been a wholly unpleasant one. But then, man does possess a remarkable facility for blocking out his bad times and only remembering the good. I had always felt a sense of security in the knowledge that I would be returning to Stoke after each weekend at home but now, I was to be at home for an indefinite period, when I would no longer have the companionship of others in a similar state to myself.

What was I going to occupy myself with? Would I perhaps be able to cope with the numerous difficulties involved with holding down some sort of employment? Would my mother be able to manage with the incessant work loads of continually putting me to bed and getting me up each day. I had additional concerns for Mum, particularly in respect of my occasional incontinence concerned problems. Perhaps, more to the point, how long would I be able to remain at home before my parents considered it time to have me committed to an institution for the rest of my life?

Numerous such questions passed through my mind during the journey home and I eventually concluded that the best thing to do was to forget about my worries and just deal with problems as they arose. If I had a full year at home, well, that was a year of happiness numerous other cases hadn't even been given the chance to have, as so many find themselves in circumstances whereby they have to enter directly into institutions after discharge; and if it was stretched to two years, that was all the better.

My mother had previously agreed that I could stay at home for as long as she was physically capable of coping with me. I have no doubt that many other mothers (or husbands or wives) have had their loved ones living at home with them for varying amounts of time under the same terms. When she, or they could no longer cope, our bags were to be packed and we were to be shipped off to wherever there happened to be a vacancy.

I'm pleased to be able to report that brother David went without his cigarettes, throughout the journey home and for that I was eternally grateful. It was a strange journey because I had now become accustomed to living in the Buckinghamshire countryside and was now heading for Hackney, a very busy and condensed borough of London. I suppose this realisation revolved around the fact that this final journey home, may be permanent would be no going back. The journey was quite enjoyable with plenty of loud pop music, on route.

As we approached home all of the surrounding streets seemed to bring back my childhood memories. I was strangely being reminded of my paper round, working on market stalls and of course my school days. David had updated me on the completion of all the alterations at 12, Aspland Grove and of course ' the social scene, in and around our street, in Hackney. It was a very different journey to the one taken in the opposite direction 26 months previously. I'm referring of course to my flight in the Helicopter, which in hindsight was so very, very surreal. As we parked outside our house, I was met by Mum who had a smile of contentment on her face. David then assisted me into my wheel chair and pushed me into my new ground floor bedroom, which had all been prepared nicely for me.

Although feeling very tired it was lovely to see my other brothers and sisters, namely Michael, Raymond, John, Patricia and June. My Dad also of course welcomed me home, but as was his way, he soon retired to the peace and quiet of his bedroom. In recent years Dad had become rather reclusive and evidently had reached the stage in his life

where he would avoid his rather large family. I had
no explanation for his unusual behaviour and soon
accepted it as the norm. I should add that I had
been Dad's favourite prior to my accident, but this
changed significantly after the accident occurred.
He was so shocked by what had happened to me,
that he actually stopped communicating with me.
This may seem strange to the average person, but it
is true. Furthermore, he never visited me at Stoke
Mandeville Hospital, during the whole of my
twenty six month's of treatment. I had done my
Dad no wrong during my life or my recovery
period, he just couldn't accept the outcome and
degree of damage I had sustained. People clearly
deal with such situations, in very different ways.

The day after my discharge, many friends and
neighbours kindly visited our house to greet me.
Several of my relatives also visited, when
convenient. I was of course delighted to see them
all. It was of course wonderful to have some more
home cooking by none other than Rose Rine, my
simply amazing Mother. My new bedroom was
proving to be well equipped and pleasantly
constructed by the local authorities. It was good to
be home at last.

Early Home life.

What happens to you after discharge depends, to a certain extent, on your physical ability and where you are living. The majority of cases return to home life, with parents or with ones husband or wife. I shall therefore deal with the difficulties of obtaining equipment and what there is to be done etc. and cover the material on employment prospects and life in institutions and homes in later chapters.

The hospitals almoner should have sorted out any housing problems with the housing authority prior to discharge. We had turned down offers of four unsuitable houses and we had our back room kitchen converted into a bedroom, with access to the garden being obtained via the installation of a set of French doors and an external ramp. The work had kept me at Stoke for over a year longer than necessary, but it was worth it.

This photograph was taken at the rear of my home in Hackney, in the summer of 1970. I'm depicted seated in my wheel chair, on the left hand side of the photograph, with brother Michael standing to my rear, holding my beautiful niece, Nicola. Yes, amazing as it may seem to be, the sun is shining upon all three of us. I'll leave you to decide who is the better looking of the three of us.

We were not in need of a hoist for getting me in and out of bed as my mother had been taught how to accomplish this by means of her executing a 'cervical stand'...and neither were we in need for a hoist in the loo as bowel evacuations were carried out on disposable incontinence sheets in bed. Our

bathroom was at the top of the house, which
necessitated me being given blanket baths, we
therefore did not need a hoist there. Evacuations,
condom urinal changing, bathing and dressing
were all carried out by my mother, therefore, we
didn't have to wait behind the street door every day
for the imminent arrival of the district nurse. A
nurse is available on request, as are home helps,
but they are often more trouble than they are worth
and if your parents or husband or wife can manage,
its the best way to get on with things on your own
and stick to a routine.

Those in need of household aids, such as
bedroom and bathroom hoists, beds and bedding
etc. should contact their Area Health Authority
(addresses obtainable from the almoner prior to
discharge) or your Social Services Department.
Depending on where you live, either might be
responsible for various services, such as the
collection of soiled incontinence pads. Further to
this you could contact The Disabled Living
Foundation or The Central Council for the
Disabled. Both have a vast amount of information
available in booklet form dealing with all subjects
related to life for the disabled so any problems

should be referred to either of these bodies for their guidance.

Joining the Spinal Injuries Foundation can also be helpful, there is also the Scottish Paraplegic Association, The Scottish Information Service for the Disabled, The Liverpool Aids Centre and the Welsh Council for the Disabled.

In my case, I couldn't go out to work as I considered incontinence, transport difficulties and being paralysed in the hands effectively put it out of the question and I therefore had to amuse myself to pass the time. Being so physically limited made it difficult not to become bored and cabbage-like in the early years and my pursuits were, TV, Radio, Hi Fi and Reading.

Reading eventually got hold of me and for a few years I was reading book after book for perhaps six hours a day, week in and week out. Many local libraries run a home delivery service for the disabled, although, since having moved into the suburbs it occurs to me that this service might only be available in the larger towns and cities. Where I live now, in Hertfordshire, there is no delivery service for the disabled and the and the mobile library which visits the area is of little use as their choice is limited and you have to rely on a third party to do the leg work. I have taken to buying all my books as I take an occasional fancy to those which are reviewed in the press.

Cards, draughts, dominoes and chess, could be played if you could obtain an opponent and in this respect I was very lucky as a fellow cervical, a Turkish Cypriot lad lived just around the corner. Oddly enough, we had seen each other in Stoke, but as his English vocabulary was then very limited we hadn't spoke and it wasn't until almost a year after discharge that we became acquainted. He had been in England for just one week when he sustained his injury by executing a deep dive into the shallow end of a swimming pool at Luton, Beds.

We were able to meet fairly frequently and we were therefore able to entertain ourselves with constantly playing cards or chess. Whenever we weren't competing we could readily discuss the physical and psychological frustrations common to the two of us. Now I have moved out of London, however, we only get to see each other every three or four months, but as he has since married, this is quite reasonable.

Generally, during the early years I would often sit through the days hoping to arrange for a pusher or a driver to take me out in the evening or at the weekend. Apart from this there were only two other means for being gotten out of the house. A trip once or twice a week to the local welfare day centre or a trip to the local hospitals physiotherapy unit, for a standing session.

In fact, the welfare centre was, and probably still is a place designed for the accommodation of elderly people, as the paralysed and disabled people generally have only been brought out into the light of day over the past decade and this being the case, the local welfare authorities haven't quite gotten around to knowing what to do with the paralysed or disabled.

Ironically, the paralysed people attending such a centre will be doing so because they are to severely incapacitated to hold down a worthwhile job of work and they will therefore be attending in the hope of discovering something adequately interesting and rewarding to do in place of their boredom at home. But, they will almost certainly be given basket making or weaving to do, which they will very likely be incapable of doing anyway as they will probably be cervical cases who are paralysed in the hands.

In the eyes of the supposedly knowledgeable members of staff running these places, the accidentally paralysed appear to be only partially paralysed; similar to multiple sclerosis or muscular dystrophy therefore all that has to be done for them to 'improve' their grip is to get on with the remedial exercise the hands will receive when persevering with the wonders of basket making etc. Yet, it is the case of nine cases out of ten that there is no grip in the hands to improve upon and all the remedial exercises under the sun are not going to regain any gripping ability as the trouble is not with the hands but the spinal cord nerves in the neck.

My mate and I didn't particularly wish to continue with the joys of basket making and we therefore had to campaign to be brought into the welfare centre via the borough buses on the same day, as previously, even though we only lived a mile apart, we were in on separate days as we were officially in different areas of the borough. We eventually brought the officials around to having us picked up on the same day. We then remained upstairs on our own, playing cards or chess, although we eventually fell prey to more cards than chess, until, after about two years of this, we became so fed up, we stopped attending the centre altogether.

I'm informed that the situation is very similar in the welfare centre were I now live and although there is a day work centre this place only has soul destroying work layed on such as that of packing numerous items into boxes etc.

I was being stood up regularly twice a week by my two elder brothers, but they eventually became so fed up with this weekly chore that I arranged to be taken into our local hospitals physio department once a week by ambulance. It was the same hospital I had been in over two years earlier when I first had my accident and as many of the staff wanted to know what had become of 'the chap who went off in the helicopter' I felt like quite a celebrity.

We had been using my plaster leg supports for standing at home and I continued to use these at the hospital. However, the staff were wholly inexperienced at standing cervicals, they quickly became worn out with holding me up and the other patients were being neglected because of me. So it was at my instigation that a tilting standing frame was eventually obtained. They would lie me out, strap me down around the knees, hips and chest and then wind it up to the vertical position, where I could remain for the necessary quarter of an hour or more for kidney drainage etc. without them getting worn out or the other patients being neglected. I could pass water freely whilst up and be easily lowered down to a lesser angle if I happened to become giddy.

I was stood near to the departments entrance and I was therefore open to wisecracks from every Tom, Dick or Harry entering or leaving the department. Still, this did provide me with an opportunity to chat with members of the general public, something not normally done at that early time. It became evident that most people just couldn't understand why such a healthy, whole-bodied looking young man had to have physiotherapy at all, let alone his having to be strapped into such a macabre looking contraption as the standing frame.

It was rather exacerbating meeting people of the 'faith healing school' who continually wished to impress upon me the need to 'have faith' when it was more than abundantly clear to someone such as myself that all the faith under the heavens was not going to cause a spinal cord lesion to be healed.

I should have attended the hospitals physio department two or three times a week for standing, but, the London Ambulance Service was so bad in picking me up late and taking me home late that a once a week trip was all I was prepared to endure. Hospital waiting rooms and corridors are notoriously draughty places to have to sit around in without having to sit and wonder where the hell the ambulance has gotten to when the physio staff, the nursing staff and in particular, the transport staff have all left the department at five o'clock sharp. During the summer months it was not to bad, but in the winter with the cold, and early darkness, waiting in a deserted, dimly lit room, until after seven or eight could be trying in the extreme.

When a crew finally arrived, it was no use moaning at them as it was the whole poorly co-ordinated system which was at fault. An ambulance crew would drop a patient off at the hospital and then be told to pick another up from the other side of London because they happened to be the first crew free, so it was no wonder patients such as myself had to wait around for such long periods. A new system was adopted shortly before I moved out of London, but it appeared to be little improvement on the previous one as I was still being left late before being picked up.

Officially, chair-bound cases were to be taken out of their chairs and put on a stretcher, but as I didn't stand and waterworks have become detached in the lifting, I was allowed to remain seated in my chair between the two stretchers. As far as I was concerned, this was by far the easiest way to travel, as I could hold onto my chair back handles for support, whereas, being sat on a stretcher would have very likely seen me on the floor with any heavy braking or cornering.

Although there are ambulances with tail lifts these are not designed for the transporting of chair-bound cases, but rather for the easy loading up of people who, perhaps had some difficulty in walking. Chairs couldn't be taken on these lifts adequately, anyway, and I therefore think it is a sorry state of affairs when a city as large as that of London has no well designed vehicles for the safe transport of chair-bound cases.

The ideal mode of transport would be a small van (for perhaps four to six chairs) fitted with a tail lift, to prevent the crews from straining their backs with the 'humping' which has to be done at present; and of course, the main feature inside should be a robust system of anchors for securing the chairs to the floor of the vehicle. Oddly enough, a vehicle I have travelled in, was designed for the transport of chairs, but whoever designed the floor anchoring system couldn't have had a clue what he was doing as the fittings were all back to front and it took the crew ten to fifteen minutes to discover a way of holding the chairs down. It was as big as a house moving van and it could only take two chairs at a time and they said it cost about ten thousand pounds; What a waste of the tax payers money.

In London, the taxiing around of out-patients was carried out by a number of ambulance crews especially picked for the job, whereas, in the suburbs, as there are less people being driven around to and from hospitals, this job is carried out by the emergency accident vehicles. These vehicles haven't any tail-lifts. Their chassis level is about two foot off the street and even before they could lift me in, not an easy task, they had to turn one stretcher up side down on the other stretcher as there was insufficient room between the two stretchers for my chair. There were then no floor anchors and I had to attempt to prevent the upper stretcher from falling on top of me whilst my chair was skidding all over the place with the vehicles braking and cornering. But, after almost two years of my wrangling with the ambulance authorities, they finally managed to obtain a suitable vehicle....brought in from ten miles away from where I live.

Employment Prospects.

Generally speaking, there are three categories one will come under with regard to any employment prospects ... the back case, who can and should work; low lesion cervicals, who can or could work under the right conditions; high lesion cervicals, who, on the whole are unable to work. Although there are exceptions to these rules.

Life should present few problems for the average back case, since the basic requirements will be an accessible place to work and a suitable mode of transport. Light bench work in a factory or some form of office work can be managed and therefore, assuming an accessible building will eventually be found, I shall continue onto the transport question.

Ideally, a saloon car adapted to hand controls should be obtained, which can be either a manual or an automatic, depending on which you can afford...the only difficulty arising is the fact that a hand operated clutch control makes driving a manually geared vehicle that much more difficult than an automatic. A saloon is easy to get in and out of, the chair can be lifted into the back seat and your family or friends can go with you in the vehicle. After the car has been adapted to hand control you can obtain a government grant towards the conversion costs from the department of Health and Social Security (which I will deal with more fully in a later chapter) and after you have passed a standard driving test an annual allowance towards the petrol and running costs can be had on request from the same department.

However, if you are unable to afford the purchase of a saloon, you can fall back on a government supplied three wheeled invalid carriage (or, noddy car, as they are called), which can be applied for via the same offices. But, for anyone who does have to make use of these carriages, I feel I should point out that it was the publicly expressed opinion of the late Mr Graham Hill (former formula one racing champion) that these vehicles are notoriously unstable to drive; and furthermore, it is the generally accepted view of the people at present using them that they can be downright dangerous to the occupant under certain road conditions.

Some of the low lesion cervicals are able to hold down full or part time jobs, but the problems involved with them doing so are far greater than those of the back cases although the basic requirements of accessible place of work and a suitable mode of transport are the same, The type of work will most certainly have to consist of some form of office work, due to not having any grip and therefore, assuming an accessible pace of work will eventually be found, I shall continue with the transport problem.

The only means of transport which can be driven by a low lesion cervical is that of a hand controlled automatic saloon...when again, once the conversion has been completed and a standard driving test has been passed (not an easy task) you will then be eligible for the conversion cost grant and the annual running costs allowance.

However, if you cannot afford to purchase a saloon, I'm afraid the prospects of being able to get to work will be severely curtailed, unless of course you can arrange for regular transport with a friend or relative. A low lesion complete motor power cervical is incapable of driving a government three wheeler., due to their controls being wholly inoperable without the use of grip in the hands.

The problems confronting such a low level cervical are further aggravated by the fact that he has to have a third party attending to his evacuations and dressing needs etc. prior to being able to go off to work on time. On evacuation mornings there is this time consuming chore to be dealt with, which can take up to three hours and than you have to be dressed. It has been suggested to me that the bowels could be cleared out in the evenings, but, alas, this is not a very viable proposition as it is highly desirable that nothing should be eaten during the two or three hour period prior to you taking an aperient, as the laxative needs eight hours or so to do its job. Doing evening evacuations would necessitate you taking your last meal around noon time, and I can't see people putting up with that year in and year out.

Nevertheless, if the cervical can arrange to have all the necessaries sorted out in time and arrange for transport then he/she can hold down a job of work; although, I agree that the strain on the people getting him/her ready and off to work can be very trying at times. Still, my c6/7 friend manages so good luck to anyone else.

For cervicals without triceps and wrist flexors, work is almost certainly out of the question, as the problems involved with getting up and off to a place of work are accordingly magnified with the greater degree of paralysis. Although, of course, I'm aware of the fact that there are cases in existence who are almost completely paralysed and who are holding down full time occupations, but these are very much the exception.

If a cervical without triceps were to hold down a job, perhaps some form of executive or managerial position, he/she would have to have an accessible place of work, someone with transport to get them to and from work and someone to deal with evacuation and dressing needs etc....from about five thirty in the morning on at least two days a week. However, you might want to have some form of outdoor work brought in....if you can find anything suitable. But, this kind of home employment is usually so repetitive (such as the typing out of thousands of addressed envelopes) that it is just not worth the effort for the mere pittance you are likely to receive in remuneration.

But, if you happen to be a vociferous reader, there is always the leisurely employment in being a publishers proof reader.

When I first returned home I contacted the Disablement Resettlement Officer (DRO) at our local Department of Employment who in fact, was of very little help. Perhaps no small wonder, considering I'm in the 'no triceps' bracket, as above.

People who were professionally employed prior to their accident may well wish to return to their old job, if this is the case and they are perhaps encountering a few obstacles, then they might do well to contact The Association of Disabled Professionals.

Children of school age, should, of course resume their schooling if possible and to this end their parents or guardians should apply to their Local Department Of Education's Stationary office for List 42, a list of schools for handicapped children in England and Wales.

For school leavers wishing to finish their education there is the sheltered accommodation available in such places as Banstead Place; and applicants need to apply to Banstead Place, Park Road, Banstead, Surrey.

Those wishing to take teacher training courses should write to the Central Register & Clearing House, 3 Crawford Place, London, W1H 2BN.....giving details as to the extent of your disability. Further to this any budding academics can write for the booklet, 'Access to Universities & Poly-techniques for the disabled, 34 Eccleston Square, London, SW1 VIPE, where numerous other booklets on the subject can be had.

Finally, for those who are unable to get out to work or attend university etc. there are Open University Courses which can be done in your own home. Of course, you will be unable to attend the two week summer seminar held each year, but it is not a necessity to obtain a degree. The people on the staff are very helpful to their disabled students so anyone interested should apply to The Open University, P O BOX 48, Bletchley, Bucks.

Institutions and Housing Projects.

Numerous cases find that they have to enter an institution directly after discharge. There are a wide variety of places which accommodate the disabled in general, but as we are basically concerned with the paralysed I shall deal with three examples, although there are many others and cover housing projects for wheelchair users at the end of the chapter.

As it is, it is incontinence problems which prevent a greater number of paralysed people being accepted into a wider variety of homes, because the people in charge of such places state that they cannot, or will not cope with incontinence cases in their care. Yet, the fallacy here, concerning the accidentally paralysed, is that they do not go about having haphazard bowel and bladder lapses as is apparently thought, as their incontinence is well controlled. Although, I would be amongst the first to admit that accidents do occur.

The Star and Garter home, overlooking the River Thames from Richmond Hill, is for ex servicemen. There are 200 beds spread throughout nine floors, each of which is accessible via a large lift There is a physiotherapy department, a small hydrotherapy unit, and an occupational therapy department that are in use by the chair-bound, which accounts for over half of those living there. The residents (they dislike being called patients) are cared for under the auspices of a Commandant, who is a doctor himself who delegates to a matron and her nursing and auxiliary staff, who are also supported by a maintenance staff. The home is independent of the National Health Service and therefore residents have to pay for their services and all donations are accepted with open arms.

As the majority of the men are ex servicemen, they are all virtually financially independent as most were awarded life pensions, which in itself, is a good thing as there is actually no worthwhile work laid on for anyone who might have been able to earn some cash anyway. However, as I've now chatted with quite a few of these chaps, they seem to be passing their time quickly and pleasantly enough without there being any work. They are happy and that must surely be a rewarding compliment to the staff who are running the place.

The Duchess of Gloucester home (known affectionately as D.O.G. house)is administered by the Department of Employment, specifically for paraplegics who are able to look after themselves and who are expected to be able to get out to work. Applicants can either deal with their local Disablement Resettlement Officer....to be recommended to the selection board or can write direct to the manager at Duchess of Gloucester House.

Much wider renowned than either of the two previous examples are the world famous Cheshire Homes. They take in incontinent paraplegics and quadriplegics-and they were started up almost accidentally by Captain Leonard Cheshire. He nursed a friend at Le Court, Hampshire until he died of cancer in 1948. The precedent having been set, the homes rapidly proliferated in numbers throughout the country, until today, there are over seventy in the U.K. and many more overseas. The actual inception of opening a new home has to be instigated by the wishes of the local community but all of the homes in the U.K. are registered under a charitable trust known as The Cheshire Foundation Homes for the Sick. Anyone who is perhaps considering the founding of a new home in their locality should contact The Secretary of the foundation.

The actual siting of a new home should be considered first as its relative position in the community can contribute to the projects being a success or failure. Admittedly, some of the buildings were donated and therefore, there was no choice as to where they were to be sited. If a home can be built within the reach of the local shopping centre, pubs, cinemas, bingo halls etc. it will make for a much happier home as the residents will not feel cut off; particularly since many homes do not have resident transport and have been opened in the middle of nowhere. I know of three such homes.

Probably the next most important point is for a happy, out-going matron or charge nurse to be found as it appears that miseries emanating down from 'the top' seem to have a depressing effect on the staff and residents as a whole. Some individuals still believe that the disabled should be kept out of the limelight. Whereas others openly put themselves out to thrust them into it and it is this difference in attitudes which can make or break the spirits in a home.

Today, more and more young accidentally paralysed people are entering into these homes and it seems to be that the homes are being increasingly geared towards catering more for the needs of these younger people, although, of course, this doesn't mean that they are being geared in this way to the exclusion of any older residents. There is very little to be done during the day apart from a little O.T. or painting and reading etc., whereas there is plenty to be done in the evenings in the way of TV, pubs, clubs, cinemas, theatre and restaurants and the like. To this end, thank god, the management are coming around to thinking that an adequate night staff should be employed for putting people to bed whenever they are ready to go.

Previously, quadriplegics, who are incapable of putting themselves to bed, had to be put into bed between nine and ten before the staff went off duty. For most youngsters, early to bed and early to rise, is just old hat and for quadriplegics in a home, where there is nothing to do during the day and everything to be done at night it couldn't be more so. In Douglas House home in Brixham, South Devon, they had an adequate night shift staff but in Seven Springs in Kent they had an inadequate night shift staff and the difference in the atmosphere of freedom in the Devon home was amazing.

Unless you are financially independent, your Social Welfare Officer will have to negotiate to get you a place in a Cheshire Home. The welfare will then assess you to discover just how much, or how little they are prepared to contribute towards the weekly upkeep. If it is then seen that you can contribute very little, or nothing at all, the welfare will then agree to meeting your bills prior to your being allocated a bed for the usual one month probationary period. However, if you have capital in excess of £1200 you will be expected to pay the full weekly bill (anything from £45 to £70 a week). Until such time as your capital has dwindled down to this mark.

A reassessment is then made and you are expected to contribute to the weekly upkeep on a decreasing scale, until such time as the capital amount is negligible, when the state will then meet the full weekly cost. However, personally, I believe this idea of depleting your capital is wrong, as after the capital has been used up you become entirely dependent on the state. A much fairer system would be to have the individual pay whatever amount they could from the interest they are making from their capital investments and in this way they would be able to contribute towards the weekly upkeep for the indefinite period.

Once in, the majority of residents are given £2.50 per week by the local Social Security Office, as in fact very few people entering such a home have any capital to worry about in the first place.

With this 'Princely' sum they are expected to meet the costs of the numerous extravagances they may wish to splash out on , such as women's make up, or a drink or smoke for the men, although I should mention that people in the home are allowed to keep the recently introduced £5.00 per week, 'mobility allowance' money. But, even with this fiver thrown in this is a scandalously low amount for one to have to live on each week(a round of drinks can cost two or three pound at a time) even considering that everything else is found. There is an annual clothing allowance (ten pound I believe) for those who are modest enough to ask for it, but, this is nothing nowadays and I think the Minister for Social Services should see to it that the present £2.50 allowance is doubled or trebled to give people a modicum of self respect, if very little else.

Perhaps the greatest need of an individual living in a Cheshire home, is to be able to get away from the home to have a holiday. This presents a greater problem than it at first might appear to, as there are very few holiday centres which cater for the incontinent. But, I understand that the Cheshire Foundation are now lessening the difficulties of where to send their incontinent people for a holiday as they are now introducing a holiday exchange programme within the homes. This provides a list of seventy possible places in which you might arrange to have a holiday. This list could be virtually doubled, if cultural exchange holidays were to be arranged with Cheshire homes in other countries.

In the meantime, however, for those residents who are fed up with holidaying in other homes, there is an excellent holiday home near Southend on Sea, Essex, called Lulworth Court, which does cater for incontinence cases. You are made to feel absolutely at ease there by the full time nursing staff and voluntary helpers. If you wish to arrange a fortnight there you need to contact the Queen Elizabeth Foundation, Leatherhead, Surrey.

As a last point, for those who are actually outside of, but sympathetic to, the Cheshire Foundation as a whole, there is an excellent quarterly magazine, the 'Cheshire Smile' circulated from the Green acres Cheshire Home. It is an informative production and can be subscribed to yearly. It is also good value for money.

Apart from the three examples of residential care given above, there are housing associations carrying out purpose built housing accommodation projects for the chair bound. They are carrying out housing programmes in various parts of the country. If you are interested you can discuss this with your Social Worker.

Lastly, there is Thistle Foundation, Edinburgh. A settlement consisting of purpose built housing for married disabled with accommodation in a hostel for single disabled. Numerous local hospitals now have purpose built accommodation for the young disabled and many local councils also build special sheltered houses and flat lets, so to find out where these places are within your locality, you should contact your Social Worker.

The Financial Situation.

Whether you will live like a king or a pauper after having become paralysed, depends on the circumstances under which your injury has been sustained. In my case, I was very 'lucky' as I was able to sue a third party for negligence and I shall therefore deal with the question concerning compensation first. My family didn't even realise that we could literally sue someone over my accident until they happened to discuss the question with a more knowledgeable cousin of mine.

Then, later on, I found myself feeling rather guiltily embarrassed over our actually taking legal action against someone whom I knew and respected. But, as my solicitor was quick to point out, it was not a personal thing but simply the correct procedure for setting about gaining financial compensation which might be due to me. However, although he stated that it was his professional opinion we had a sound case for going to court, he added that I shouldn't build up any grand hopes over being awarded a fortune overnight., since, even if the case was eventually presented to a judge, the whole rigmarole of compensation awards was such a lottery that I, the plaintive, could all to easily come out the loser.

Unless you happen to be financially independent, the first hurdle to overcome is that of proving you have a sound case for taking before the courts, before the local area Legal Aid Board (there are twelve such boards nationwide), will grant the necessary funds for covering the costs of the legal fees it will take for the case to be duly prepared and taken before the High Court. At the outset, perhaps it would be best to contact your local Citizens Advice Bureau to help in attaining legal aid.

I was eventually awarded full Legal Aid after it was seen my parents couldn't possibly afford to take the case to court themselves. The Legal Aid was then dragged out for four years before we were supposed to have our day in court. But, alas, we didn't actually get our day in court as, after a great deal of haggling, I accepted a settlement out of court on my solicitors advice. Having signed away all my rights of appeal, I've forever since been wishing we'd taken the case before a judge whenever I read some of the handsome rewards being made today. Nevertheless, a bird in the hand is certainly worth two in the bush; and as my solicitor stated on subsequent occasions, I could easily have ended up with nothing had we gone into court, in the event of the judge having gotten out of the wrong side of the bed that morning and perhaps discovered a minor flaw in my case which was not altogether legally sound.

It is undoubtedly a fact of life, that if you are going to sustain a broken neck or back it should definitely be sustained whilst involved in a road traffic accident , since it is when a spinal cord lesion has been had under such circumstances that the most generous compensation awards are made in court. However, in the past, there were numerous spinal injury victims who found that they couldn't receive a penny in compensation, as they had sustained their injury when they were involved in a road traffic accident which they had caused themselves whist only being insured for third party claims. Now of course, vehicle occupants have to be insured so this situation can no longer arise.

At the present, going rates in the 'High Court Compensation Stakes' race, a' back case' could be expected to receive around £50,000 and a 'neck' around £80,000, although these figures should not be accepted as being exactly what every back or neck case will automatically receive, as they are figures which I have averaged out for either category based on cases successfully brought before the courts in recent years. Some will be awarded to much and others will be awarded to little, most of the time. Although, since it can take from one to ten years for a case to be eventually be heard, when an award is finally made it is definitely accepted with open arms, as by that time you are worried about not being awarded anything at all.

The amounts awarded are calculated to provide you with a capital investments income comparable to the income you were earning or may reasonably expected to have been earning, had the accident not occurred. This method of calculating awards makes it very difficult for the solicitors involved to agree on an amount that, say, a school-age child accident case should or should not receive. There are so many points to be included to be included in their estimation as to the child's lost potential earning capacity, that a case can never arrive at a figure which he or she could expect to receive, even if, or when the great paying out day arrives.

Then for every case that is widely publicised as having received a handsome amount, there are perhaps a half dozen or so other cases we don't hear about in which a small or no award at all had been made. Of course, you can appeal to a higher court, but it would appear there is very little compassion to be had higher up as all judges must necessarily make their judgements within the strict letter of the law, when, even though a judge may feel that a given case deserves an award on moral grounds, he will be unable to award anything unless the individual concerned has a water-tight legal case entitling him or her to such an award.

When cases are compared the anomalies brought about by the method of calculating awards stand out in stark reality. A man earning £80 per week was awarded £74,000 and a man earning £30 per week was awarded £30,000. Yet the man awarded the lower amount had a family twice the size of the other mans and he was much more severely paralysed. Two other cases, concerning a young man and a young woman were in the news recently because they had both been awarded compensation by the courts. They had both been involved in road traffic accidents in which the drivers were not insured for passengers. So, the lad was awarded £18,000 to be paid off to him by his friend, the driver, at a rate of £2 a week (180 years of payments) and the girl was awarded £50,000 to be paid off to her by her driver, at the rate of £5 a week, (200 years of payments).!!!!

Currently, the whole question concerning whether or not any given case will receive due compensation or not is certainly a lottery. If you can afford to hire a top solicitor and barrister all will eventually be made to turn out well.(as in three such cases I'm acquainted with). Whereas, if you have to rely on State Legal Aid, pressures can be brought to bear for you accepting a quick out of court settlement under circumstances where a case is perhaps dragging on to long and the legal costs are mounting dramatically.

The method of calculating compensation is wrong and I believe a much fairer deal could be had all round if a State run Compensation Board were to get set up, to award people amounts based upon the degree of their paralysis, say £50,000 for a back and £80,000 for a neck (since most back cases can still work), with the awards being made automatically, irrespective of who was or was not, responsible for the accident occurring. After all its bad enough being paralysed without having to put up with years of legal wrangling to add to your lot.

Almost on a par with rewards made through the courts is that of compensation awarded by the Industrial Injuries Benefit Scheme, paid to workers who have sustained their injury at their job of work. They are either paid a lump sum gratuity or a weekly pension, although, I do know of a Scottish man who was awarded both. On the whole, the lump sums are not as generous as those awarded by the High Courts, but are usually sufficient enough to leave a person with very few financial worries.

When an injury has first been sustained, you should apply to the local Social Security Office for payment on a weekly basis. Until after twenty six weeks, when it is seen that the paralysis is of a permanent nature. The person dealing with a given case should arrange for it to be brought before the Industrial Injuries Board for an assessment to be made. Again, the awards are worked out on the basis of what you were or might have expected to be earning, and there are therefore numerous injustices created, as opposed to the much fairer deal which could be had if awards were made with regard to the degree of your paralysis i.e. back or neck case.

In fact, not all industrial workers are covered by the scheme, as those who injure themselves whilst being self employed in sub-contracting work cannot claim compensation under the injuries act. A young man I met on ward 3 in Stoke Mandeville, had sustained his broken back whilst engaged in his trade and he should definitely have received compensation, irrespective of whether the small print on the Act covered self employed subcontractors or not.

The most lucrative condition under which you should preferably sustain your injury is whilst being on duty in either of the armed forces. You are pensioned off for life on a full pay pension, the higher the rank the more you will receive each week. There is the added advantage that your pension is reviewed whenever the forces pay is reviewed. However, we are again faced with an anomaly since an officer will be receiving a higher pension than a recruit, when the officer could be a back case and the recruit a neck case.

The unluckiest set of people sustaining a spinal injury are those who have no other person to blame but themselves (and this group includes the majority of all spinal injury cases), when they have had very little or no accident insurance cover. Then, unless you are able to work, state aid has to be applied for via your Social Security Offices. Although people can and do manage to cope on such meagre benefits they often have to exist on a standard of living which is actually less than half that of the national average.

Supplementary benefit can be applied for in cases of obvious hardship and a rent rebate or subsidy can also be had. But, as there are so many combinations as to an individuals circumstances and the payments he or she may or may not be eligible for, the best course is for you to ask for a home appointment visit from a Social Security Officer, who will explain your entitlements in detail. Further to this, if you feel you are not receiving your due entitlements you should contact the Disablement Income Group who will assist you.

The recently introduced Constant Attendance Allowance has helped boost the income of the non working paralysed, although this has only raised their income to slightly above half the national average. There are two categories under which you may be entitled, the day only allowance, for those in need of daytime attention and the twenty four hour allowance for those in need of both day and night attention. A quadriplegic should be entitled to the full allowance, and a paraplegic to the day only allowance, although you can apply for the full allowance on the off chance that you may get it. Your GP has to endorse the application form and it is then up to the Attendance Allowance Board to decide whether or not you are entitled to anything.

But, as with any government financed boards, the usual amount of red tape has been layed down for the board members to adhere to. It is therefore advisable for whoever happens to be filling out the application form to include an impressive array of medical details as can honestly be put down. All the powers of heaven and earth cannot possibly cause the boards decision to be reversed. The full allowance is £10.60 and the day only allowance is £7.60 per week.

A non contributory Invalidity Pension Scheme has now been introduced for those who have never worked and who therefore never had the chance to pay into a sickness and pension fund with stamps. Payment is at the rate of £7.90 a week and anyone wishing to apply for this pension should obtain the booklet to get the relevant details.

Transport.

For numerous paraplegics and quadriplegics without any transport of their own, getting about to places that are not within easy pushing distance (other than the welfare day centre or hospital physio department... when transport is laid on),can present one hell of a difficult problem. Bus travel is absolutely out of the question, as there is nowhere for stowing a wheelchair, even if you were prepared

to carry it on and off. Taxis and mini cabs are not a very desirable
 means of travelling since the majority of drivers are reluctant, or downright unwilling to waste their time with lifting you in and out of the car and a wheelchair in and out of the boot. Tube train travel is virtually impossible (even in the cities that have them) as there are very few accessible stations.

For longer journeys, main line trains could be made to be more readily usable to the chair bound. If the numerous sets of stairs which confront you at almost every station were to be supplemented with a lift, the present carriage doorways were widened to allow access to someone seated in a chair, as opposed to the present situation whereby the chair-bound have to travel in the guards van and if corridors were widened to allow the chair bound access to the dining carriage and toilet.

However, British Rail have recently brought into service a number of first class carriages with a removable seat for accommodating a wheelchair user. You should give British Rail 48 hours notice if you intend to make use of this facility and only second class fare is charged for the first class carriage. The trains can only be taken from Euston, Stockport, Manchester Piccadilly, Watford

Junction, Runcorn, Macclesfield and Liverpool Lime Street Stations at present, although the service is to be extended in the future.

When travelling abroad you are confronted with the many problems of air travel for the chair-bound. There is first and foremost the trouble with actually getting to the airport, with being lifted in and out of cars or on and off of trains. Once there, the airport authorities frequently insist on you using their decrepit wheelchairs for being pushed across the tarmac whilst your own chair is being stowed. Then there is the messy business involved with being taken out of the chair , carried up the steps and plonked into a seat, although there are occasionally co-operative officials to be found, who will arrange for you to be put aboard seated in your wheelchair via a lift or forklift truck, if you happen to be incapacitated enough. But you still have to be lifted into a seat once aboard.

For everyday transportation, private vehicles are the answer although from what I know of the transport systems which are currently being envisaged by technocrats the world over, chair-bound people are not going to be getting around anywhere in future since the common auto mobile is going to be replaced by various systems of tracked computerised matchboxes, which are anything but accessible to a wheelchair.

Nevertheless, we are free from these systems being brought into service for a decade or two yet and after having received my compensation money, I was able to afford the purchase of a Ford Cortina Mark III, four door, automatic saloon. My friend and I had to be content with attending the welfare centre and hospital physio for the previous four years with their transport and so the car came as somewhat of a sanity saver, at that time. We knew I might encounter some difficulties with driving but we also knew that he would be able to drive even if I couldn't.

The car had to be converted to 'hand' controls first and I rang three different firms to discuss prices There was a vast difference in prices. I opted a firm who ensured me I would be able to manage without a power assisted unit and an appointment was arranged for the car to be taken in six weeks later as there was a long waiting list for conversions, even though the firm was reputed to be converting some fifty vehicles a week.

Well, the time came and went and I was duly wheeled out to inspect the work four days after the appointment date. Being an automatic, only the brake and accelerator had to be fitted up for 'hand' control, and for ease of steering I'd had two bobbles fitted on the steering wheel... one at twelve o'clock and one at six o' clock. Numerous cars can have a dual control accelerator and brake mounted in one lever on the steering column, but alas, with the ignition being housed on the steering column in my car, the accelerator could only be mounted there and the brake control had been brought up through the floor on an extended removable lever, just to the drivers left leg. The controls were rather unsightly and tended to rattle a bit but these defects were negligible after you had gotten used to them.

When applying for a provisional driving licence I filled out all the disability declarations on the form (there was in fact, no reference to quadriplegia) putting paraplegia to the question asking for the nature of my disability, since I saw no point in getting the bureaucrats at County Hall flustered with a discussion as to whether or not a quadriplegic could be legally granted a driving license. To my great delight, I was issued with a licence a fortnight later.

Actually, getting insured presented a few headaches. At the onset my insurance agent didn't know if we could be legally insured without having any grip in the hands, he didn't know whether or not we could get provisional licences, at that time and he didn't think his company would insure us at all, let alone send us an estimate of the premium. He had never dealt with such a perplexing client before, but he agreed to send off the application forms covering any driver and two disabled drivers on a comprehensive policy. He turned up three weeks later to inform us we were insured. The points system had knocked the cost of insurance up to £175.00 but if that was to be the cost of us having a shot at driving I was prepared to pay it. However, this amount was eventually reduced to £130.00 after he had informed me that you get a 20% reduction on the first year of the 'no claims' bonus system and then £120.00 after I'd agreed to pay the first £25.00 towards the costs of any minor knocks or scrapes the car might get. I gave him a cheque and he issued a cover note and my friend and I were free to drive.

Well, we were each having driving lessons whenever we could arrange for a qualified driver to go with us, as there are in fact, no driving schools for quadriplegics. I had to be lifted in and out, I couldn't steer around corners adequately enough (as only half a revolution could be turned, with the crook of my wrist on each bobble before having to let go and bring my wrist to the next bobble). My arms became easily worn out (due to lack of muscle control), and I could not brake effectively enough for an emergency stop, when having to use the brake lever with my weaker left arm.

After some thirty lessons I had to drop the idea of my being able to drive and that is why I stated earlier on that driving was out of the question for cervicals without tricep control, unless they happen to be incomplete motor power cases or they can afford to have a car thoroughly adapted to their needs regardless of costs. My friend carried on having lessons, however, and I sat back looking on whilst cursing myself for not having broken my neck an inch and a half further down.

Previously, I had sent off to the Ministry of Health & Social Security in request of a £90.00 conversion costs grant and having forwarded my log book, insurance cover note, provisional licence and a bill from the firm who did the conversion for me to prove the car had been converted, I was awarded the full grant. In fact, £45.00 was toward the cost of the controls work and £45.00 was the cost of having your car converted from manual to automatic. Even though mine was automatic, I was allowed to have this money anyway.

When the cheque arrived there was some literature from the department informing me that a disabled person driving his own car was eligible for an annual £100.00 running costs allowance, but when I sent off all the necessaries, they wrote back and told me my 'provisional' driving licence did not entitle me to the grant. Well, by that time I had given up being able to drive and so, when my friend eventually passed his test, I sent his driving licence off asking if we could have the annual allowance on the moral grounds that there were two quadriplegics using the one car, making it doubly justifiable for us to be entitled to the money. But, alas, they sent back stating that his licence didn't qualify my car for the allowance.

They sympathised but, I could not have the allowance until I could drive my own car. The rules clearly stated etc...etc...It did cross my mind to sign my car over to my friend but I wasn't prepared to go quite that far to obtain their silly grant.

A qualified disabled driver can obtain a road tax exemption certificate from the same offices. A privileged parking badge can be obtained through your Social Services Department. Although there are some places you cannot park and the leaflet you receive with the badge will explain all this to you.

At present, a paralysed person has the 'choice' of having a three wheeled invalid carriage (if they can drive one) or the running annual costs allowance towards running their own car (if they can afford one and can drive it themselves) or the newly introduced £5.00 per week Mobility Allowance for those not driving a three wheeler or those who are unable to drive themselves. Most quadriplegics cannot however drive a three wheeler due to their not having grip and many hundreds without tricep control, cannot either afford to purchase a car or cannot drive one even if they could afford one.

What is needed is a small Government Supplied saloon to meet the transportation needs of those who are either unable to drive an invalid carriage or whom are unable to purchase their own car. A third party can then chauffeur these people about and the mobility allowance money can be used for running costs. A Mini can be had from the government at present but only if there are two disabled people in one household or there is one disabled and one blind person., or if there is a disabled parent who has a school age child to care for. My friend had to wait until his father went almost totally blind before the Ministry agreed to supply a car, when, shortly after having taken custody of the vehicle, his father had died and we are now expecting the automatons of the Ministry to repossess the car at any moment.

After having moved away from my friend and driver, I saw little point in keeping my saloon car and I have now replaced it with a Ford transit van, which is insured for any driver. In a way it is a great improvement on the car as the difficulties of lifting me in and out of the passengers seat and the chair in and out of the boot have been dispensed with. You could have a battery operated tail lift fitted for £60.00 or an engine operated one fitted for £150.00, or even a set of ramps could be used. Having a couple of healthy brothers on hand, we therefore managed with my being lifted straight in without more ado.

The chair was originally held in place by means of two upturned bolts and a crossbar across my large back wheels, held down with wing nuts. I then reduced the time it took to secure my chair by doing away with this anchoring system and replacing it with a single strap method of anchorage. The chair faces the rear of the van and there is nowhere it can go, even under emergency braking conditions. I maintain balance by hooking my arms around the chair handles during cornering etc. although of course, anyone above c5/6 travelling in this way would need to have some kind if harnessing fitted to keep them in their chair.

Getting out and about.

Generally speaking, whether one is young or old, single or married, or living at home or in an institution, the thing to do is to lead as full a life as you can have after having become paralysed. Of course the availability of transport can be a limiting factor on your social life. In my experience the more you get people to take you out, the more people are prepared to put themselves out to get you out a little more often. This then has a spiralling effect and before you know where you are, you have a social life which is to exhausting to keep up with.

Actually getting in and out of cars presents a problem for the weightier cervicals, but this can be overcome by means of you being gotten in and out by a third party executing a cervical stand, similar to the way my mother gets me on and off the bed. Little people can get big people in and out of vehicle once this method of transferring has been perfected. For those who find it difficult, an engineering firm have recently invented a swivel seat which can be swung out of a car door for a cervical to be transferred onto the set with a little more ease.

With transport, there are numerous things to be experienced by the paralysed. I know of two paraplegics who go sub-aqua diving, several who attend horse riding clubs and one quadriplegic who actually pilots his own glider. Although, I must confess, I do not know how he manages it. For us lesser mortals, however, there is theatre, cinemas, concert halls, pubs, clubs, restaurants, race tracks, bingo-halls, rugby, football, tennis, cricket matches. PHAB clubs (physically handicapped-able bodied), Toc H clubs, blind peoples clubs, old peoples clubs, MS clubs, paraplegia clubs etc.. etc. Anything you want to go to see or wish to do can be experienced once you, the individual, has decided not to let the grass grow under your feet.

Pubs, clubs and restaurants are available countrywide and they are usually quite accessible to a chair. I frequent pubs much more than clubs or restaurants as I find people are more forthright when they have been 'tanked up' as the saying goes and I often receive a truthful opinion as to someone's views of the chair-bound in society when such opinion is expressed under such circumstances. Occasionally I hear things I do not like. You have to be a bit thick-skinned, but on the whole it appears that the general public are all for integration with the chair-bound.

When having a meal in a restaurant it can be embarrassing, since it appears to be the case that numerous members of the public are interested in seeing just how you manage to convey the food to your mouth, but, on the whole, people are good mannered enough to avoid staring to much, even when you manage to drop a glass of wine in your lap. I've been given the impression that wheeling a wheelchair into a place, lowers the tone of the establishment a little, but, if your chair is kept clean there can be no objection to your presence and no ensuing indigestion as a result.

What restaurant managers do object to is having more than two wheelchairs in their restaurant in one party, unless it has been arranged with the manager prior to the arrival of the chairs. I once went to dinner with five other wheelchair users, when I was made to feel very uncomfortable myself with all the fuss involved with arranging the chairs around the table. So if this eventuality can be avoided it should be.

The thing that prevents many chair-bound people from attending clubs more frequently is their assumption that their presence may inhibit people from dancing. This is nonsense of course, as in fact people are actually made to feel how fortunate they are to be able to dance. I have been asked from time to time if I would like to have my chair wheeled out to dance with a young lady although I have as yet declined any such offers from young women since it is this type of thing which I find distasteful.

Some of the clubs are inaccessible since they are often situated in basements and even in cases where there are not one can be carried in by volunteer from the bar etc.

The PHAB clubs are a recent innovation, the aim of which was to attempt to bring about greater integration of the handicapped with able-bodied people. But, I'm afraid from what I have seen of the clubs, the idea has fallen flat as the expected, or perhaps I should say hoped for integration hasn't

come about. It appears that this is so because the
meetings are usually held in youth club centres,
where the able-bodied youngsters have come to let
of steam and they are consequently nor prepared to
just sit around chatting to the disabled. What is
needed are centres which can be attended by older
members of a community who are more likely to be
interested in furtherance of the necessary give and
take, to bring about the required integration.

Multiple Sclerosis clubs now exist in virtually
all areas of the country (1 in 1200 people suffer from
it) and if you wish you can apply to become an
honorary member. I attend my local club at each
monthly meeting and all the members are very
friendly. Outings are arranged quite frequently and
this all adds to you having a fully active social life.

Paraplegia clubs are rather few and far
between at present, probably because there aren't
that many accidentally paralysed throughout the
country as yet. Although, with the existence of the
Spinal Injuries Association something might now
be done to set more such clubs up regionally. As it
is, you will only be in the company of paraplegics
and quadriplegics if you happen to be living in a
spinal unit or in one of the sheltered housing
community projects mentioned in a previous

chapter. But then, do you need the company of
other paralysed people? One fellow sufferer can be
of great value, as I found with my association with
my Turkish friend but there is really no need to be
surrounded. To much talking about paralysis can
become very boring.

When attending the theatre or cinema you
are confronted with the ludicrous fire regulations
pertaining to the chair-bound. In London, the
Greater London Council authorities are responsible
for enforcing these regulations and they have
recently clamped down hard.

In the past the theatre and cinema managers
were prepared to turn a blind eye and allow you to
remain seated in your wheelchair in the aisle,
contrary to the fire regulations. But, since the
clamp down they now insist that each and every
chair-bound person be carried out of the
wheelchair and plonked on a stall, regardless of
whether or not you can actually sit up on a stall.
The wheelchair is taken away leaving you
absolutely stranded. The idea is that if there is a
fire, the mass of people can be gotten out quickly
without them having to clamber over a wheelchair.
But, woe is the disabled person left sitting on the
stall.

In fact, cinemas are very rarely full these days and the situation of having a fire crazed mob falling all over a huge wheelchair blocking their escape route is not likely to come about. Although, in the theatres, with the capacity audiences and very narrow aisles, I agree that a wheelchair parked in the way could be a danger in the event of a fire breakout.

However, the problem of safely seating the chair-bound could easily be overcome If the G L C and other authorities were to introduce a fire regulation rule stating that all cinemas and theatres must remove two or three conveniently sited stalls to make accommodation space for any chair-bound patrons. In this way, the chairs wouldn't be blocking an aisle and everyone concerned would be happy...including the presently stranded disabled people.

I recently suggested to my local cinema manager that he could move a couple of stalls to accommodate wheelchairs but he refused to do this as the fire regulations clearly stated that a chair-bound person could not be left sitting in their chair under any circumstances. The rules must be changed by the G L Cs upper echelons so....G L C and other authorities please note my suggestion.

For the people living within, or within commuting distance of London, there are three bonuses available in the way of entertainment, The Royal Festival Hall complex, the New National Theatre and The Royal Albert Hall.

The Festival Hall usually has three programmes each evening with the Queen Elizabeth Hall catering for minor concerts, and the Purcell Rooms catering for lectures and poetry readings etc.

All three have been designed for access to the chair-bound and the advantage of being in a wheelchair is that you can attend either entertainment for a princely sum of 25p. You can contact the theatre and be put on a mailing list to receive the monthly advanced programme list and this enables you to book up for the concerts well in advance.

The chair-bound can be gotten out of their transport at the front doors of the main building and the commissionaire will allow the transport to be left there until after the performance. Inside, there are lifts to all floors and the main bar, the sandwich bar and restaurant are all accessible to the chair-bound. There are eight places for wheelchair plus attendant and although the wheelchair area has been sited well back off the stage, the acoustics are good and each performance can be enjoyed and heard with ease. A drink can be purchased by your escort from one of the upstairs bars during the interval. A beautiful view of the River Thames can be had from a large balcony whilst you are enjoying your drink.

The New National Theatre has only just been opened and the productions are not yet in full swing. However, you can write and ask to be put on the mailing list. The theatre has a wheelchair reserve area, which is relatively close to the stage and the bars and toilets are accessible to the chair-bound.

An evening out at the Royal Albert Hall is similar to that of one at the Royal Festival Hall, except for the fact that you need to be carried up some steps to get in. Again, you can write to the hall to ask to be put on the mailing list. There are only two wheelchair places worth having, that are quite near the stage and although the wheelchair occupants are allowed in free of charge the escorts have to pay the full ticket price. The place is rather archaic, however, so the toilets and bars are not all that amenable to the chair-bound, but I have been allowed to have a drink brought into the auditorium, so there is no problem of a thirst.

As more and more of our older inaccessible buildings are modernised or pulled down and many of our new buildings are designed to be readily accessible, the quality of life for the chair-bound will become increasingly more enjoyable. Complete integration can only be brought about if the chair-bound and the disabled generally are prepared to get themselves out into public places and place themselves under the very noses of the public at large. When this is being done we shall gradually be aware of a change in attitudes, whereby, the chair-bound in particular, will be able to take part in the social life of our communities to an ever increasing extent. This is the situation which should prevail and it is the situation which, I hope and expect to be brought about in the not to distant future.

I would now like to mention some of the books that I read after returning home from Stoke Mandeville in 1969. I read 'The White Nile' written by Alan Moorehead, which told the story of the Great early explorers of Africa, including Dr Livingstone. It was a truly wonderful book which took me to a far flung place, despite my paralysis.

The characters in this true story were just magnificent, as they made their way across this very arid and dangerous landscape, in search for the source of the river Nile.

I also read ' The godfather ' the famous book about the Italian Mafia. This was also a very interesting book packed with the true stories of brutal Murder and mayhem inflicted on others by The Mafia. After reading the book and realising the mortality rate in the stories, I began to realise that paralysis was not so very bad, after all.

I then read Leo Tolstoy's ' War and Peace ' the famous book about Napoleon Bonaparte's advance into Russia and his subsequent defeat due mainly to the harsh Russian winter and subsequent starvation. I found the details of the families involved on both sides of the battles very interesting indeed. The sheer nature of the hand to hand fighting of that period of world history was simply horrendous and on many occasions extremely heroic. The book included some great love stories also which helped the reader, to deal with the blood and gore.

I read many other wonderful books both whilst living in Hackney and subsequently at my new home at 127, Wheatcroft, Rosedale Way,

Cheshunt, Hertfordshire. I suppose one would say that music and reading were my main hobbies. This seems like a good opportunity to tell you a little more about our move from Hackney. Mum of course was now in her mid to late fifties and despite the alterations to our home in Hackney, in the ideal world we needed a bungalow, which of course would make life easier for all concerned.

Hackney Borough Council started to make enquiries with a view to alternative accommodation, for my family and I. Whilst this was under way, sadly my dad became ill and was diagnosed with a brain tumour. In very quick time dad was losing his speech and was admitted to the local hospital for an operation to remove the tumours. The operation went well and in very quick time dad was able to communicate normally again. Dad's recovery was going very well for a week or so, then came the bombshell. The doctor acting on dads behalf informed us that they had now found incurable cancer in both of dads lungs.

The whole family managed to visit dad in the hospital, but his health deteriorated rapidly and he sadly died within three weeks of his diagnosis. He was only sixty one years of age and had fought the hard fight, very bravely indeed. R.I.P.

It was quite difficult for my brother Michael, his wife Danusia and family, who had just moved home to Irchester, in Northamptonshire, five days prior to our dads demise. They had been unable to afford a house in London and Michael had arranged a transfer of employment, as a fitter, to The Express lift Company at Northampton. Despite being in the middle of the moving process Michael and his family managed to return for dads funeral, at Enfield crematorium, which took place late in February, 1972.

Things seemed to settle back down after the funeral and mum seemed to be coping well, with the loss of dad. Michael and Danusia had taken out a mortgage on a small house at Irchester, and all seemed to be going well with the purchase. However, Michael's employer then informed him that his transfer to The Northampton lift Company had fallen through and that the post was no longer available. Happy days!!

Michael continued working at Tottenham, London, for six months, before joining Northamptonshire Police, at the request of his wife Danusia. He did a thirteen week Initial Course at Ryton on Dunsmore, Warwickshire. He sent me a letter after the first three weeks, stating that he was struggling on the course. I wrote back giving him moral support and I'm pleased to say that he went on to complete the course satisfactorily. Clearly, I had my uses, but I must not sing my own praises!

PART FOUR. –

Book Writing

It was now June-July time-1972 and I decided to start writing ' the said book ' about my accident and my life, otherwise known as my autobiography - ' A split Second Accident '. Yes, it was tough, but my 'sturdy steed', my gifted electric typewriter, stuck to the task and my first manuscript was completed within three years. During that period of time my family and I were also offered a lovely bungalow, to live in at Cheshunt, Hertfordshire. We viewed the property and accepted it, in very quick time. It of course involved great upheaval for my family, but, ' beggars could not be choosers '

The reasons for the move were in fact two fold. Firstly, I would have a large ground floor

bedroom with a proper facility for my ablutions.
The bungalow also had good front and rear access
for a wheel chair. Secondly, Hackney Borough
Council were due to demolish the whole of Aspland
Grove. In other words-time had run out for those
living in Aspland Grove !! This was rather sad news,
because there had been a real sense of community,
in the place, otherwise referred to as the Grove.
Together with my family we soon moved to our new
address namely 127, Wheatcroft, Rosedale Way,
Cheshunt, Hertfordshire.

Obviously, there were a few hiccups, but
these were soon overcome and the family soon
settled down at the new Council Bungalow. I was
delighted for my mum because she was now ' head
cook and bottle washer ', in a large well designed
modern kitchen. It measured approximately twelve
square metres, which was huge, in comparison
with three square metres at Aspland Grove. My
younger brother Raymond had left School and had
started work in the pattern cutting trade. My
youngest brother John was still attending Senior
School, at the time of our move to the bungalow.
They now shared quite a large comfortable
bedroom. Mum now had a small bedroom which
looked out onto the rear garden.

Having completed my book I decided to contact a couple of Publishers with a view to publication. Each of the publishers were in receipt of copies of my manuscript, at which point I sat back (literally) and waited for their replies. I was both excited and quite proud of my achievement. I felt that I had given a good and interesting account of the early recovery and day to day life of a quadriplegic. I waited of course with baited breath, assuming that I would hear back from the publishers, in pretty quick time. Well, within days I had received written replies from both publishers confirming that they were interested in my book. However, both wanted a large upfront payment from me, to cover their costs for publishing my book.

I'm referring to hundreds, of pounds, which I later learned, are referred to as ' vanity payments '. I should perhaps explain that first time writers become excited when Publishers show instant interest in their books and often feel compelled to make these extremely large payments. I'm afraid I couldn't afford to pay a publisher a huge some of money, to publish my book and therefore declined both offers. My decision left a bitter sweet taste, in the mouth and it took me several weeks, to fully realise that my book may never be published, despite all of my determined hard work, on the typewriter!!

I would like to place on the record that as time ultimately progressed, I fully came to terms with the reality of the situation. It wasn't all bad news, because, whilst writing a book it can become a form of therapy. It gives you time to off load an enormous amount of sadness and stress, which you have accumulated during your years of hospitalisation. So please, if anyone out there is contemplating writing their own, don't be put off by my experience. I decided to place all of my A4 size book pages into a binder and simply leave them resting on the shelf, of the family bookcase.

Brother Michael, Danusia and their children came to visit us at the new bungalow and I'm pleased to report that tradition swung immediately into play. Within fifteen minutes of their arrival, Michael wheeled me across the road to the local ale house, where a couple of pints were thoroughly enjoyed. This was a great opportunity to catch up on day to day events and of course put the world to writes. I think the pub was called ' The Royal Oak ' but please forgive me, if I'm wrong. Due to the fact that Michael visited at weekends, the pub was at it's busiest and with plenty of customers, always had that feel good factor!!

I enjoyed a game of cards at that time, which would normally follow our return from the pub. We usually played three card brag or poker and we would often be joined by my oldest brother David. We of course played for loose change, but the kitty could on occasions reach between four or five pounds sterling. I enjoyed an occasional gamble and would also place a bet on a horse, particularly when ' The Grand National ' was being run.

My younger brothers Raymond and John were now growing up fast. Ray had passed his driving test and could now drive my Ford Transit van. Occasionally together with Mum we would all travel up to Michael and Danusia's house at Irchester, Northamptonshire, in my van, where we would enjoy a day together. It was lovely to see their children Nicola and Steven, who of course were quite young at the time. I recall visiting Wicksteed Park at Kettering, with Michael's family and enjoying a pint afterwards at a pub near to the park entrance. On one such occasion we stopped overnight at Michael's, where I slept in the lounge, in a bed fetched from upstairs.

We also visited The Bedford Arms in North Bedfordshire, where I was introduced to Green Kings, Abbott Ale and I.P.A both great tasting, hand pulled beers. Danusia went on to have a third child Ian, who was born in 1975, at Wellingborough, completing the Northamptonshire arm of our family. I was pleased for Michael and Danusia, because they now had a nice little family and seemed to be living in a nice part of the country. Well, we were soon on our way back home to Cheshunt, with me seated in my wheel chair, in the back of the' tranny ' van. I actually travelled in reasonable comfort with the wheels of my chair being firmly anchored to the floor of the vehicle.

We usually arrived back mid to late evening, at which point poor old Mum would need to prepare me for bed. Mum would soldier on regardless, despite the fact that ' although never admitted ' she was ageing fast. In truth, Mum was finding the dressing and undressing, placing me in or out of the bed, increasingly difficult. I would feel a little relieved when my two weeks holiday time arrived. Mum would prepare all that I needed for my two weeks away at one of The Cheshire homes. My favourite by far was Southend, where the home

was actually situated on the sea front at West Cliff.
Weather permitting, holiday makers like myself,
could be wheeled across the road to the
promenade, where we could sit looking out to sea
and sunbathe.

August was the best time to go to West Cliff,
where the sun would be guaranteed, at least once a
week. We could watch a vast array of ships making
their way up and down the estuary. Then we had
the typical smell of the sea to inhale and the
constant flight display, by the local sea gulls. I'm
sure you would all agree, that there is something
special to behold, when sea gulls start squawking
along the sea front. Of course we also had the
choice of an occasional burger, or an ice cream, at
the sea side. Despite being in the main old
buildings, the Cheshire holiday homes were both
large and comfortable places to stop. As with any
holiday break, time simply flew by and before you
knew it, your transport and driver would arrive to
drag you back to reality.

One thing was for sure, I would arrive home
knowing that Mum will have enjoyed her two
weeks of respite. I would of course always thank my
various family drivers for conveying me back and
forth, for my holiday. Again, with the help of my

drivers, I was able to visit Longleat Safari park, Whipsnade Zoo, Woburn Safari Park, and many other places of interest. These day trips out were also very much appreciated and definitely helped a cervical case, in keeping one's sanity.

Mum had further respite when my annual check ups were due, at Stoke Mandeville. The check ups consisted of a whole week's admission to the hospital ward, where a very detailed series of tests and examinations would be carried out. The procedures were to ensure that a cervicals general health was being properly maintained whilst residing at home with your family. I had now completed 6 annual check ups, since being discharged in 1969, all of which had passed off without any problems. Some might say ' What more could my Doctors wish for ' I was clearly, the perfect cervical patient.

Time was now flying by and my next check up was due for the second week of June, 1976. I contacted my friend Turan to let him know that I would be away for the week. We were good mates and were both in the rather good habit of keeping one another informed, as to what was going on, in our rather hectic lives. Well, all the normal preparations were made and before I knew it, I was off to Stoke Mandeville, for my latest check up.

Raymond drove me to the Hospital and after saying our goodbye's, I was taken to the ward where with help, my personal items were placed in the bedside cabinet. Every time that I returned to Stoke Mandeville for my annual check up, I always felt strange, probably because most of the staff and the patients had moved on. However, after a nights sleep I would awake with renewed confidence and crack on with the necessary check ups. These included blood and urine tests, followed by thorough examinations by the specialist doctors, as to my general fitness and well being.

The time was passing quickly and I recall my brother Raymond answering the phone when I rang home on the evening of the 10th June. We had a chat for about twenty minutes and I explained that everything was moving along smoothly, during my treatment. I reminded Ray to purchase a pack of lagers, in readiness for my return home, at the weekend. Mum also came on the phone and I took the opportunity to tell her that all was going well and reminded her that I loved her. After further routine attention by the nurses and the duty orderly, I retired to my bed for the night.

PART FIVE.

–

Tragedy Strikes.

Disaster is about to strike.

I am Alan's older brother Michael and it now falls to me, to tell you what happened next.

During the early hours, of the 11th June, 1976, my wonderful brother, Alan, had a massive heart attack, whilst in his hospital bed. The nursing staff fought a hard fight to save him, but despite their best efforts, he was pronounced dead, by the duty doctor.

He was only twenty six years old and in my humble opinion, 'a hero'.

As a quadriplegic he had fought a hard fight for nine years and never once held anyone to account, for what had happened to him. Despite the huge disappointment, that he had suffered at the age of seventeen, he just got on with life, despite the cruel hand that he had been dealt.

He was a wonderfully unselfish person, which is evidenced time and time again, during the writing of his manuscript. Nearly every paragraph contains information which would have helped other cervical patients with their recovery, during the late sixties and seventies. We know that he was in essence turned down by publishers and that his manuscript had been left on the family book shelf. Sadly, Alan's manuscript sat on the family book shelf, gathering dust for many years and I will explain what happened to it later.

The tragic news of Alan's death was of course conveyed to mum and family at Cheshunt, who were of course in great shock!! I was then told on the phone what had happened and of course my wife and I were very shocked and hugely saddened, by this very upsetting news. I spoke to Mum on the phone and did my best to support her in which ever way I could. It was very difficult however, due to the distance between us, but my brothers and sisters were there to support her. Mum requested that I make contact with the hospital, for identification purposes and to make any necessary arrangements in respect of Alan's sudden death. Although I wasn't looking forward to this task, I did in fact feel honoured to be going to the hospital, on Mum's behalf.

I was granted one day's compassionate leave from work and was soon on my way to Stoke Mandeville, arriving two hours later. As arranged, I made my way to the administration office, where I liaised with The Coroners Officer and The medical Staff who were dealing with Alan. I enquired as to why Alan had sustained a heart attack at such a young age. The Medical staff explained that cervical cases were always under threat of heart attack, due to damage caused to their vital organs during paralysis. Furthermore, that quadriplegics could suffer more heart attacks, due to their sad lack of everyday exercise. I of course understood what was said and later conveyed all the relevant information to Mum, during my next phone call home.

I was told that Alan's body was awaiting my arrival in The Chapel of Rest. I steeled myself and made my way via the long corridors, to The Chapel of Rest. I new exactly where it was, because I had passed by it, many times before with my brother in his wheel chair. The hospital chaplain was standing waiting for me at the door of the chapel. After introductions he showed me into the chapel where I could see my brother Alan layed out in a coffin. The chaplain said "take your time, I'll see you later" and then he left Alan and I alone. Alan looked at peace and had one eye partly open, which pleased me, because I felt that he was saying his goodbyes.

I remained in the chapel for about thirty minutes and recall touching Alan's forehead, which was stony cold. It was of course a touch of affection, it was the least I could do on behalf of my family. I spent the half hour reflecting on our childhood together, the times when we were both fit and able, to run together. Although I had four brothers, I looked upon Alan as my little brother, I was the second born and Alan was the third. Most children naturally tend to look after their younger brother or sister. I found myself telling Alan how much I loved him and I then literally had to force myself to leave the Chapel of rest, via the single entrance door.

I returned to the administration office, where being the next of kin, I identified my brother Alan's body to the Coroners Officer. I was then asked a number of funeral related questions, which I answered on behalf of my mum Rose. I was given a number of Alan's personal items of property which were to be handed to mum at a later date. It was decided after a short discussion that in Alan's particular case, a Post-Mortem would not be necessary. It was thought that nothing would be achieved by carrying out a Post-Mortem. I was pleased with this decision because I didn't want my brother ' to suffer ' any further disruption to his body.

Having been given a detailed explanation as to how Alan had died, I'm able to say that I drove back to Northamptonshire in a much calmer frame of mind, than when I had earlier arrived at the hospital. Alan's body was later conveyed back to Hertfordshire, in readiness for his funeral, which of course was carried out by local undertakers, at Cheshunt. I recall very vividly the amazing array of flowers, that family and friends sent for Alan's funeral. They were all laid out on the grass verge to the rear of mums bungalow and simply glowed in the bright sunshine, which had been gifted to Alan, for his special day!!

Alan's service was held at Enfield Crematorium with the whole family attending, with many friends and acquaintances also present. It was a splendid service with many fitting tributes being paid to Alan. A wake took place back at Mum's bungalow which passed off very nicely indeed. At a later date Alan's ashes were placed in our Dads plot at Enfield Cemetery, together with his name plaque. I feel proud to be able to say that Alan was very sadly missed by all of his family and friends.

I knew that future visits to the family home in Cheshunt, were never going to be the same again. My brother Raymond seemed to be in a daze because Alan had relied heavily on him when transport was needed. I remember more than most, that Ray took many months to come to terms with the void in his life. Mum on the other hand had been relieved of her twenty four hour duty of care for Alan and seemed at ease with her new found freedom. Clearly, she had loved Alan dearly and had shown him complete devotion, during his nine years of paralysis.

The simple truth, was that her age and general fitness left her struggling to keep up with the day to day grind involved in looking after Alan. Mum had developed lower back pain and also suffered with arthritic pain, both of which, made her tending to Alan's everyday needs, more and more difficult. Putting it in simple terms, she was a hero, who never once complained about the day to day caring of her son Alan. All mums do what mums need to do!

I had began to sense that Alan had concerns about mums physical deterioration. He did in fact comment one day that he was considering the idea of moving into a Cheshire home, with a view to full time residential care. Alan's untimely demise on 11.06.76 had of course changed everything, in one foul swoop. On a bright note, mum was now seeing improvement in her lower back and week on week, became more energetic. Mum was now nearly sixty years of age and some might say that her improved health was as a result of ' divine intervention '.

I struggled to come to terms with Alan's sudden loss and found myself searching my mind for a way forward, without him. Two weeks prior to his death, I decided to give up smoking sixty cigarettes a day. I had been smoking for fourteen years, initially Golden Virginia tobacco role ups and then embassy- tailor made filter tipped cigarettes. Despite all the stress involved with giving up smoking, I decided that I would never, ever smoke again, in memory of my beloved brother. I'm pleased to say that I have not smoked a single cigarette since making my promise and feel deeply indebted to Alan, for the good health that I have enjoyed to date. As a result of my promise, I will have stopped smoking for a total of forty years this coming May. I've always been of the view, that Alan's loss, was my gain! I'm convinced that had I not stopped smoking in 1976, I would have followed in the footsteps of my Father and have died, early, in my life.

Raymond continued working successfully in the pattern making industry and later managed to buy an apartment in Enfield, London. He later settled down with his girlfriend June and went on to purchase a house in Enfield.

John went on to study several ' A ' level examinations successfully at School and after six years at Medical School, obtained two degree's. He went on to become a very successful Doctor, in

Kent, where he now lives with his wife Sue and their four daughters.

Our sisters Pat and June both married and moved away from the family home, both successfully having children. Pat spent a lot of her spare time looking after mum and often invited mum over to her house at Chingford, Essex, where she would stop over, quite often. Pat had a lovely house at Chingford and I know that mum really enjoyed her visits and really felt at home there. Pat devoted a lot of her time to mum and I for one, thank her for that. Whenever I visited mum at Pat's house, she always seemed contented and was no doubt pampered.

Mum eventually ended up residing in her bungalow alone and enjoyed many more years of reasonable health. During mum's early working life she had worked for many years on a sewing machine, linked to the rag trade. The many years of treadle work had left her with a very damaged knee joint, which culminated in knee surgery, in her seventies. This did not bode well for Rose, due mainly to the effects of the anaesthetic, which later caused the onset of Alzheimer's. Rose eventually had to move into a residential care home at

Buntingford, in Hertfordshire, where she remained for three years.

The whole family visited Mum regularly, but sadly, as time passed, she was unable to recognize any of us. Mum lived until she was eighty one and passed away, peacefully, at the care home.

Buntingford was a beautiful little village and I particularly recall my family and I, pushing mum around the village, in her wheel chair, prior to her passing. In accordance with mum's wishes, she was cremated, with her ashes being deposited in the same plot as dad and brother Alan. It was a very sad day indeed when mum departed this life, but I personally felt that she was finally at peace. Alzheimer's certainly seemed to be a cruel end, for such a hard working and loving mother.

Prior to mum's passing, I had shown an interest in Alan's manuscript and informed Mum that I would like to look after it on her behalf, with a view to seeking publication some time in the future. Mum agreed that I should take his manuscript back to my home in Northamptonshire, where it could continue to gather dust on my book shelf Well, Mum wasn't wrong because the manuscript remained on my book shelf untouched from the late seventies, right through to 2015. It was in fact early in 2015, when I decided to read and update Alan's manuscript.

I personally found it to be a fascinating story, much of which I simply had not been aware of. I had not read it properly, my only excuse being that I had raised a family of my own and had been very involved in my Police career. I feel a little ashamed of myself for having retained Alan's manuscript for over 35 years, without doing anything with it!! I feel sure that my mother would be unimpressed with my sad lack of effort, during those 35 years. However, in 2008, I felt the need to revisit Stoke Mandeville Hospital, with a view to reliving some moments of family history, in respect of my brother Alan.

I spoke to Danusia and explained that I needed to spend a day of remembrance at the hospital and she agreed to come with me. I had been retired for eight years and realized that I had several goals, which I needed to achieve at the hospital. After the passing of time, I wanted to visit The chapel of rest again and reflect back to my visit in 1976, when of course thing's moved at a rapid pace!! I was no Longer tied to a days compassionate leave by my employer. I would be visiting in my own time, which somehow seemed important to me.

I also wanted to see the massive improvements, that had reportedly been made to the hospital, as a result of charitable donations, by a now disgraced individual, by the name of Jimmy Saville. Danusia and I set off early, on a beautiful summers day and arrived two hours later. We visited The Chapel of Rest and paid our respects. This was followed by a walk throughout the hospital, where I could see huge improvements, when compared with the Nineteen Seventies. The most obvious improvement related to the many corridors, which had been widened, properly interconnected and carpeted, wall to wall

We visited a couple of the wards and found that they had been fully modernized. Suffice to say that they now had a more inviting feel about them, despite the fact that seriously injured patients were still in abundance. A new canteen had been built and appeared to be very comfortable for both patients and visitors. Danusia and I had a hot meal which was wholesome and enjoyable. Then came the ' Deja-vu ' moment, when a young man aged about 16 years entered the canteen in a wheel chair. He appeared to be a cervical back case and manoeuvred his chair to the adjoining table. A couple who appeared to be his parents then joined him at the table, for lunch. His father was unable to find a chair, at which moment I did my good deed for the day and handed him mine. It left me feeling that I had helped ' a little ' at their time of need.

I remember leaving the Hospital at about 3pm with a view to beating the beginning of the rush hour traffic. I felt very contented because I had been planning my visit for many years and had finally got round to actually, doing it. It was now the thirty second year of Alan's passing and I felt that I had now paid my respects to both him and this world famous hospital. The journey home took just over two hours and I recall feeling that our visit to the hospital had lifted a great weight from my shoulders. Danusia and I agreed that our visit had proved very therapeutic. I have had the misfortune to visit a lot of hospitals in my life, but Stoke Mandeville is by far ' the most humbling ', in my opinion.

I would now like to explain what I decided to do with Alan's original manuscript. As indicated earlier, 2015 had arrived and it was time to ' move with the times ' and transfer Alan's work, onto our computer, with a view to editing and preparing it, for publication. Additionally I felt it necessary to explain how Rose and the remaining family members coped, after Alan's sudden demise. I must confess that I found the task of rewriting Alan's story very upsetting, particularly when he sat and cried, when moved suddenly from one ward, to another!!

Alan highlighted a number of problems out in the community, experienced by Wheel chair bound individuals, of his time. He clearly had great foresight and would be delighted if he could see the modern day improvements, that have been put in place for disabled people. I suppose mobility scooters would be one example, although some pedestrians would disagree. He would have been impressed with the two man mobility scooters.

Internet Technology is now massive and I'm sure that Alan would have thought it a wonderful invention, particularly, when used by disabled people. He would also have been very impressed by the equipment that is now available for paralympians. I must confess that I have been a bit of a ' Dinosaur ' with regard to computers, but very much appreciate what can be achieved, when surfing the net.

The R.A.F. Rescue helicopter.

Whilst working on Alan's manuscript I decided to go onto Facebook and catch up with a group called ' Our Childhood in Hackney ' 1940 to 1970. Members of the group regularly added interesting stories about various locations in Hackney, relating to a variety of socially interesting subjects. These would include schools, parks, cinema's, youth clubs, sporting facilities, many pastimes and occasionally, subsequent employments. One particular day, my attention was drawn to an entry by a man named ' Ken Jacobs ' who told the story of working as a porter at Hackney Hospital.

I'm unable to explain why, but I found myself immediately warming to this individual, by the name of ' Ken Jacobs '. Having stated that he worked as a porter at Hackney Hospital, Ken then included several minutes of 'Cine' footage, which showed him and a colleague clowning around in the hospital grounds. It was very entertaining, particularly when one of them acted out the role of a waiter, who served up pig swill on a dinner plate to the other porter. The clowning continued for a few minutes and it struck me that these young men were going through a period of stress relief, probably during their ' tea break '.

An interesting parallel for me of course was that this porter Ken was working in the wards, at the same hospital, where my brother Alan had been admitted. I decided to send Ken a message, to establish whether he had been working at the hospital during 1967 and furthermore, had he met my brother Alan? To my complete amazement, Ken replied very quickly indeed and said that he had met my brother at the time of his admission, to the hospital. He said that he remembered that Alan had sustained a serious neck injury at his school gym. He said that he remembered the patient being treated at the hospital for several days, before it was decided that he would be transferred to a specialist hospital, for ongoing treatment.

Ken then formed part of the team that escorted Alan by ambulance down to the local playing fields, for his ongoing helicopter trip to Stoke Mandeville Hospital.

This was simply wonderful for me to be
speaking to this man who had actually played an
important role, in my brothers transfer from one
hospital to another, so many years ago. Ken then
dropped another bombshell by stating that he had
actually cine filmed my brother, being transferred
from the ambulance to the ' chopper '.
Furthermore, that the footage of the transfer,
formed part of the earlier mentioned cine film
which, Ken had put on Facebook, only recently. As
soon as our conversation ended, I viewed the cine
footage and saw Alan being carried from the
ambulance, on his stryker frame, by a team of
medical staff. Whilst viewing the footage, I found
the experience to be very emotional. It was quite a
shock to see live footage of your beloved brother,
39 years after his sad demise.

The medical team were then seen to carefully
load Alan and his stryker frame into the helicopter.
The Police and Fire brigade were all in attendance,
assisting with the unusual procedure and of course,
safety procedures! You may recall Alan referring to
the Helicopter dipping forward, as it started to take
off, well, that's exactly what I observed whilst
viewing the footage. Although rather sad, I find
this footage very interesting and once again in my

life, I find all the emergency services, to be, just fantastic! You may also recall Alan congratulating the Pilot, on his expertise during the flight, in 1967.

Photographs.

I have extracted a number of photographs from the cine film, one of which shows that it was an ' RAF ' Rescue type helicopter, which Alan was probably unaware of at the time. I think that this is a wonderful part of the story, because Alan had hoped to join the RAF and could well have done so, had it not been for his colour blindness.

When viewing these photographs, please accept that the quality is limited, due to the fact that they have been extracted from 60's cine film. They are, however, sequential and therefore a much valued record of transfers, from ambulance to helicopters in the 60's. I have included foot notes with each photograph, in order to highlight details, which I feel are of particular interest.

Prior to the series of air rescue photo's, I will now mention an old family photograph of the first five children. Alan is situated on the left hand side, with David to the right and I'm far right. June is situated at the front middle position with sister Patricia to the right.

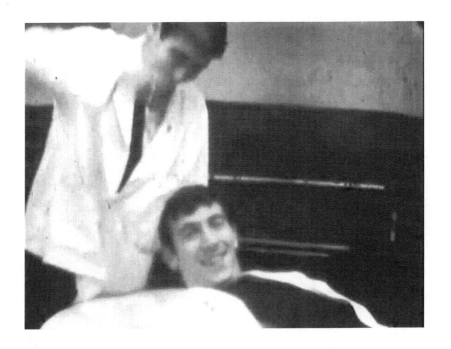

Here we have Ken Jacobs in the prone position, apparently being treated by his friend, another hospital porter.

Ken of course is my hero, being the person who recorded all this information on his cine camera, in 1967.

I'm gaining the impression that hospital porters thoroughly enjoyed their work.

Here we have the ambulance parked on the playing field and you can see the helicopter's rotary blade at the top right side of the photo. A Police officer is standing to the centre of the photograph, with his helmet raised aloft. You may recall that Alan mentioned the local press being in attendance, well, you can see them milling around in this photo.

I find this photo to be very interesting, recording the smoking flares on the left, which I assume are there to assist the pilot to land the helicopter, safely. We also have a fireman to the right of the photo, wearing a typical fireman's helmet. Clearly, safety was very much in evidence, with all aspects of the emergency services in attendance.

We now have a great view of the helicopter with a member of the crew standing in the open doorway.

The crew member has now alighted from the helicopter and is being approached by people assisting in the transfer. I find myself thinking ' what a beautiful machine ' that has landed safely, to assist my brother. The earlier mentioned rotor blades can now be seen very clearly, stretching out, above the roof of the helicopter.

You probably noticed on the previous page that the ambulance has clearly moved closer to the helicopter and the ambulance doors have been opened front and rear. I'm sure everyone would agree that the helicopter looks a little sad, from this particular angle. People are gathering in readiness to transfer Alan from the ambulance to the helicopter. This of course would have been a very delicate procedure indeed.

The ambulance team, assisted by others, are now seen to be carrying Alan towards the helicopter. You can see that he has been wrapped in blue and brown blankets. You can also see one of the grey coloured straps, being used to secure Alan to the stretcher. It hardly seems possible that this actually happened 50 years ago. I feel that the trees in the background confirm that this was winter time. I'm unable to recall the exact date. For me, the face on the helicopter again looks sad, with it's bottom lip hanging down.

The team are finally easing Alan and his stretcher through the helicopter door. It makes me feel very proud of our emergency services and of course the helicopter crew.

We can actually see one of the helicopter crew on the left hand side of the photo, who appears to be wearing a yellow life jacket.

Alan has now been placed safely aboard the helicopter and we now see the words RAF RESCUE painted on the side of the helicopter. The crew member with the life jacket is now seen leaning into the helicopter doorway, probably checking the security of his or her latest passenger.

The ambulance has moved away and the field has been cleared. An RAF crew member is returning to the helicopter which is now preparing for take off. Shortly after this cine film moment, the helicopter

took off and landed safely at Stoke Mandeville
Hospital 15 minutes later.

I must take this opportunity to thank Ken
Jacobs again from the bottom of my heart, for his
cine film and these wonderful pictures.

This photograph shows the modern look of Stoke Mandeville Hospital.

This photograph relates to 4 large pieces of stone situated at the main entrance to the hospital. They refer to 4 principals, namely determination, courage, inspiration, and equality. I feel that my brother Alan achieved all of these goals, during his short life time. This hospital, in the author's humble opinion, must rank as one of the best in the world.

I feel that I have now come to the end of Alan's story and hope that when finally published, people embrace it, as I have.

As his brother, I often wonder how his life would have panned out, had it not been for his very traumatic accident. Armed with his ' A ' level results, I'm sure he would have gone to university and eventually achieved a very successful career.

In memory of Alan I have recently placed a granite bird bath in my rear garden. I did this with two reasons in mind, in memory of Alan and my love of birds.

Although now, a rather old story, I really hope that people find it of interest. I'm sure that the treatment of quadriplegic patients has improved enormously since Alan's split second accident.

Acknowledgements.

Posthumous thanks to Alan Robert Rine for his enormous effort in typing his original manuscript.

Posthumous thanks to his Mother Rose Rine for her dedicated help and support during Alan's 9 years of Quadriplegic life.

Enormous thanks to The NHS. For their support when dealing with the accident in 1967 and treatment both at Hackney and Stoke Mandeville Hospitals.

Special thanks to Uncle Harry.

Special thanks also to Ken Jacobs for his help and photographs.

Thanks to my wife Danusia for her help in Publication, after the sad loss of our intended Publisher, Mr Richard Cowley. R.I.P.

Last but not least, I wish to thank the Printers for their work on this book and their help after the sad loss of Richard Cowley, on 5.1.17.

Details of the Printers are recorded on the Copyright page at the front of the book.

I must also Thank The R.A.F. For their Helicopter Rescue work in 1967, relating to the flight from Hackney to Stoke Mandeville, which of course was very much appreciated by my younger brother Alan.

THIS BOOK HAS BEEN PUBLISHED IN MEMORY OF ALAN ROBERT RINE, WHO TRAGICALLY LOST HIS LIFE, FAR TO EARLY.

I WISH TO PLACE ON THE RECORD, THAT I BECAME THE AUTHOR, PURELY DUE TO HIS PASSING. IT HAS BEEN A REAL STRUGGLE WITH ONE'S EMOTIONS.